PATH UNGUIDED

Grieving Your Father's Death

BALD SOLOMON

Bald Solomon recognizes and sincerely thanks the members of his creative team, including Kameron Williams, Trisha Fuentes, Laina Grote Adams and Kelly Grote. This book would not have been possible without their combined talent and work.

ISBN: 978-1-962821-09-4 (Paperback)
978-1-962821-03-2 (Ebook)

PATH
SERIES™

CHAPTER 1

The best way to deal with losing someone is to honor and preserve their memory.

Delilah Boaz perched on the edge of her porch, her eyes locked on the city of Mount Moriah as it shimmered in the distance, its lights a sprinkle of artificial stars. The sun was setting, casting a warm orange glow over the horizon, and the air was thick with the scent of honeysuckle and freshly cut grass. A chorus of cicadas filled the evening air, punctuated by the distant barking of a dog.

"Delilah!" Her father's voice boomed from inside, pulling her mind from the beautiful scenery. "You still have that report to finish for the company!"

Delilah rolled her eyes, then got to her feet with a sigh of resignation. She had been dreading the conversations she and her father had been having lately about the plant. Everyone in town knew that Alexandria Meat was in the middle of an acrimonious dispute between management and the workers, and Delilah's father had been adamantly supporting management's desire for greater profitability rather than the requests for better working conditions from the workers. Delilah knew her father cared about the workers, but he also cared about the company's bottom line in a way that made him appear cold. All he seemed to talk about lately was making more money, and Delilah found herself increasingly troubled by his stance, especially when it ran contrary to what she believed was fair and just.

As she stepped into the house, she braced herself for another round of arguments and debates with her father. He was already sitting at the kitchen table, looking over a stack of papers from Alexandria Meat marked with a highlighter and scribbled notes—all part of his efforts to make sure management had whatever they needed to win.

"Coming, Dad!" she called back reluctantly, inwardly cursing the fact that not only did she work for the largest employer in Alexandria, but she also worked for her father. *That's such a hassle.*

As head of quality control at Alexandria Meat, Delilah spent her days inspecting meat products, ensuring they met the company's strict standards. It was an important role, but it left her craving adventure and excitement outside the confines of Mount Moriah.

Delilah had begun to daydream of a more exciting life, one far from home where everyone had accents, where there was delicious food to sample and new places to see.

"Delilah, you know how important your work is," her father continued, his voice muffled through the screen door. "Without you, we'd have no idea if our products are up to par."

"Right, Dad." She sighed, forcing herself to stand and walk back into the house. She knew her father was proud of her position at the company, but she couldn't shake the feeling that there was more to life than the daily grind of inspecting meat products.

As she settled at the kitchen table, surrounded by the familiar smells of home cooking, Delilah opened her binder and began writing up her report. Her thoughts sprinted, her pen flying over the page as she detailed each inspection she'd conducted that day.

"Good job, Delilah," her father grumbled approvingly from the living room, oblivious to the turmoil raging inside Delilah.

Delilah took a break from her report and stared out the window, suddenly aware of her emotions. As the clock continued to click forward, the sun dipped below the horizon, and the world outside was cast into shadows. She longed for the freedom to explore those dark corners and uncover the secrets they held.

"Are you done?" her father asked, poking his head into the kitchen.

"Almost," she lied. "Just need to proofread it."

"All right," he said, nodding in satisfaction before retreating back to the living room.

Delilah's mind whirred with questions and doubts. Was this really all there was? Was she destined to spend her life inspecting meat products in a sleepy town that held no secrets or surprises?

Her mind drifted to trips to Europe her father had taken her on. Prague, London, Edinburg—they had all been so exciting—but Amsterdam had been her absolute favorite. She wondered if it was possible to live in one of those places—to work there for a few years and have an adventure.

As she gazed out into the inky darkness, she ached with longing. She knew she wouldn't stay in Mount Moriah forever, but what would it take for her to break free from her mundane existence and chase the adventure she so desperately craved?

"Done now?" her father asked, startling her from her thoughts.

Wow, get off my back, Dad. "Y-yeah," she stammered, closing her binder. "All done." *Done for now, at least.*

"Good," he grunted, returning his attention to the television.

Delilah stared at the closed binder, a mix of determination and fear swirling within her.

"Delilah, we need to talk!" Abe called from the living room, his voice tense and strained.

Delilah clenched her jaw as she walked in, bracing herself for another argument. They'd been at odds ever since rumors of a labor strike started circulating at Alexandria

Meat. As one of the company's quality inspectors, Delilah had firsthand knowledge of the workers' grievances. They were demanding better wages and working conditions, but her father stubbornly refused to listen.

"Sit down," he said, pointing to the couch opposite him. Delilah hesitated for a moment before reluctantly obeying.

"Your coworkers are getting out of hand," Abe said, his eyes narrowing. "They're disrupting our operations, and I won't stand for it."

"Maybe they have a point, Dad," Delilah replied, her voice barely above a whisper. "The conditions aren't exactly—"

"Excuses!" he snapped, cutting her off. "I built this company from the ground up, and I won't let a bunch of ungrateful employees tear it down."

"Is it really tearing it down if they're asking for something fair?" Delilah shot back, unable to hold back her frustration any longer.

"Fair? Who are you to decide what's fair?" Abe retorted, his face growing red with anger. "You think you know more than me about how to run a business?"

Delilah flinched at the harshness in his tone, her chest tightening with guilt. Her father had sacrificed a lot for their family and the company, but that didn't mean he was always right.

"No, of course not," she said, looking away. "I just...I see how hard they work, and I can't help but feel that they deserve more."

Abe scoffed, shaking his head dismissively. "You've always been too soft, Delilah."

"Maybe," she admitted, tears pricking at the corners of her eyes. "But I can't ignore what's happening around me."

"Then maybe you shouldn't be working for Alexandria Meat," he suggested coldly, his words slicing through her like a knife.

Delilah stared at him in shock, her pulse quickening. Was he really suggesting she leave her job, the one thing that tied her to this town and to him? The thought both terrified and exhilarated her, and she struggled to find the right words to respond.

"Is...is that what you want?" she stammered, her voice cracking with emotion.

"Maybe it's what's best," Abe replied, his gaze unwavering. "For both of us."

As Delilah sat there, her world crumbling around her, a surge of anger and determination pulsed through her. If her father was willing to push her away over something like this, then maybe it was time for her to face the unknown and finally pursue her dreams.

"Fine," she said, her voice steadier than before. "If that's the way you feel, then maybe I should leave."

Abe didn't reply, but Delilah saw the flicker of pain and regret in his eyes. As she stood up and strode from the room, she knew that their relationship would never be the same again.

CHAPTER 1

As Delilah walked away from the tense confrontation with her father, a wave of emotions washed over her. She had gone in with the hope of creating some sort of understanding between them, but instead, she was walking away feeling more alone than ever. The tears that had been threatening to spill slowly began to fall as she went to her room, and for a moment she felt utterly lost.

But then, like a beacon of light amid the darkness, one thought filled her mind: Jobe. Just thinking his name brought a warm sensation that spread a comforting embrace throughout her body. He was the one person who always seemed to be able to make her feel better no matter what was going on in her life; something about him drew her in and made all her sorrows seem less significant. Even now, when everything seemed bleak and uncertain, he remained a constant source of comfort. Delilah smiled as images of Jobe filled her with a sense of peace.

Desperate for a distraction, Delilah grabbed her keys, got in her car, and drove over to Jobe's house. *I hope it's okay that I'm coming unannounced,* she thought as she pulled into his driveway.

She got out of her car and nervously walked up to the front door. She knocked.

She heard movement from inside, and then Jobe opened the door, his golden retriever puppy, Smokey, frolicking at his feet. "Hey, Delilah," he said warmly, his deep voice calming her jittery nerves. "Come on in. What's going on?"

"Not much," she replied in a small voice, stepping inside. "I was wondering if you wanted to head to O'Malley's? You know, like old times?"

Jobe paused for a moment before responding. "Sure, that sounds great," he said finally. "Let me change into something a little more presentable." Jobe shuffled off to his bedroom.

Delilah smiled with relief as Smokey jumped on her legs, his front paws barely touching her knees. She petted the fluffy puppy all over, grateful that Jobe had agreed to go out on such short notice. After Jobe had changed, they headed out the door, and Delilah was determined to make the most of this unexpected evening out with Jobe.

When they arrived, they found a corner table in a dimly lit pocket of the bar. Delilah ordered a pint of beer, and Jobe chose a glass of whiskey. When their drinks arrived, they settled into their seats and sipped them slowly.

Jobe watched her closely, no doubt noticing the sadness that seemed to drip from her as sweat on a hot summer day. "What's wrong?" he finally asked.

Delilah inhaled deeply and explained the situation with her father and the conflict at work. Jobe listened intently as she spoke, his face filled with sympathy and understanding. When she finished speaking, he reached across the table and placed his hand over hers, squeezing it gently.

As Delilah spoke, a memory surfaced: the two of them sitting on the dock by the river, their laughter mingling with the sounds of rushing water. She remembered confiding in Jobe about her dreams of leaving Mount Moriah to explore the world while he shared his own ambitions of becoming a firefighter.

"Well, enough about my dad," said Delilah after a moment of silence had passed between them. "How's your dad doing?"

"He's actually doing really well," Jobe replied with a hint of pride in his voice. "He's been working on a construction site near Mount Moriah, building a small church for the locals."

Delilah smiled, happy to hear that Jobe's father Hosea was doing something so noble and selfless. "That sounds like an amazing project," she said, genuinely impressed.

Jobe nodded in agreement, a smile spreading across his face as he talked about all the progress his father had made on the construction site over the past few months. He described that they had cleared and leveled the land, laying a solid foundation for the church, and were now beginning to build up the walls and lay down shingles for the roof. Delilah was amazed by all of the hard work they were putting in, and she was grateful that there were still people like Hosea Johnson out there who were willing to go above and beyond for others.

As Jobe continued talking, the air around Delilah began to feel charged. Delilah couldn't deny that spending time with Jobe always made her feel better. They had been friends since childhood, though sometimes it seemed that they were more than that. But they had rarely talked about anything more than friendship. Now, however, with his warm hand over hers, the look of concern in his eyes, and his easy smile, it was difficult to explain how their friendship had never evolved into anything more.

As she thought this, Jobe showed another look, deeper and more intimate. *What is he thinking?* Their faces drew closer as if attracted by some form of magnetism, closer and closer, and she couldn't even help it.

She felt his breath on her face, a soft breeze caressing her skin. His eyes were full of affection and understanding—the same look he always had when they talked about their dreams and hopes for the future. The space between them grew smaller and smaller as their faces drew nearer until, finally, she felt his breath on her lips, a whisper of possibility.

But then the door of the pub slammed shut, startling them both. Jobe immediately pulled away, and Delilah looked down at her drink, embarrassed.

Delilah's cheeks flushed as she stood up from her chair. "Well, it's getting late," she said quietly.

Jobe nodded, and they both stood up, exiting the bar without another word.

Jobe drove them back to his house, and then Delilah got in her car to leave, wrapping Jobe in a quick hug before she went.

Delilah felt a strange mix of emotions as she ventured home. She fluttered with both excitement and fear, her skin tingled from the warmth of Jobe's hand, and she couldn't stop smiling. She had never felt this way before, and yet somehow, it was so familiar. The road seemed to stretch on forever as she drove back toward Mount Moriah, but no matter how far she went, the feeling lingered with her, a pleasant reminder of all that had just happened between them.

She was lightheaded with anticipation as images of their almost-kiss filled her head and kept replaying in her mind. *What an evening!* Delilah was overwhelmed by the power of that moment—the intensity, the intimacy, the potential for what could have been… It left her feeling hopeful for what might come next.

But that same thought also made Delilah nervous. If their friendship did evolve into something more, would it still be as special? She was already so used to the comfortable companionship they shared, and she feared that the introduction of romance could change everything. Plus, if things didn't work out between them, would their friendship survive the test?

Delilah's mind filled with questions and worries as she drove on through the night. But despite all of her worries, she couldn't deny a slight hint of excitement in her stomach—could love really be on the horizon?

When Delilah made it home, she paused on her porch for a moment to take in the evening sky. She heard sirens and a commotion in the distance but ignored it in favor of contemplating what had just happened with Jobe at the bar.

She was still uncertain what it all meant, but one thing was certain—there was something between them that couldn't be easily explained or denied any longer.

But as the sound of sirens grew louder, a tinge of cold gripped Delilah as she looked out into the twilight. She could feel that something terrible had happened as the siren's lights flashed ominously through the newly dark sky.

Then she heard the thudding of frantic footfalls, the panting of heavy breath. Her father, Abe, was running up to the porch.

"Delilah!" Abe called, breathless. "There's been an accident at a construction site!" And he pointed behind him where red siren lights flashed through the evening air. "It's Hosea!"

"Jobe's dad?" Delilah questioned, remembering Jobe telling her that his father was building a church.

Delilah's stomach dropped, and her eyes widened in horror. Her mind immediately began spinning out all the possible scenarios of what might've happened to Jobe's dad. Her stomach churned with fear, and her hands began to tremble uncontrollably. "I was just with Jobe," she told her father. "What's happened?"

She instinctively reached for Abe's hand, turning to see police cars speeding toward the scene of the accident, their sirens blaring against the night air.

"Is he all right?" she demanded, searching her father's face for any clue she could find.

But what she saw on his face was a grimness she had never seen before.

Abe's brows were furrowed in a deep frown, his lips pressed in a solemn line. His usually bright eyes had gone dull, filled with an intense look of concern. He let out a heavy sigh and shook his head slowly as if unable to form any words that would adequately answer her question.

The blood drained from Delilah's face, and her stomach dropped with dread as reality set in—whatever happened at that construction site was far more serious than she anticipated.

"Is he all right?" Delilah asked again, even more demanding than before.

Her father's eyes were wide to the whites, nothing but fear and sadness showing in them.

CHAPTER 2

The wind howled as it tore through the graveyard, whipping up leaves and dust. Jobe Johnson stood at his father's graveside, staring blankly at the dark mahogany casket that held the remains of the man he had known his entire life. The sky was an angry gray, threatening to open up and unleash its fury.

As the pastor droned on with the eulogy, Jobe tried to hold back the tidal wave of emotions that threatened to consume him. His hands shook uncontrollably, and tears welled in his eyes, blurring the world around him. He blinked hard to fight away the tears—but they wouldn't be held back.

Hot tears streamed down his face with abandon.

The reality of the situation was too much for Jobe to comprehend. His father had been taken from him in an instant, and he couldn't believe it. He wanted to shout out in anguish, but instead, he bit his bottom lip until it drew blood. He felt so helpless and weak. How could this have happened?

Jobe tried to take solace in the fact that his father was at peace now, but deep down, he knew that wasn't enough.

He'd never get to hear his father's stories again or see his smile light up the room when he walked into it. Jobe felt an emptiness inside him, a void that could never be filled again.

He tried to think back on all the happy memories with his dad and cling to them for comfort, but they seemed so distant now—merely a dream that had faded away as soon as he woke up.

"Jobe," Jonathan whispered from beside him, resting a hand on his shoulder. "You don't have to speak if you don't want to."

But Jobe knew he had to. He owed his father that much. Taking a deep, shuddering breath, he stepped forward, feeling every eye on him. The thick grass beneath his feet seemed to protest with each step, making it harder for him to move.

"Um," he began, his voice cracking under the strain of his grief. "My father…he was an incredible man. He taught me everything I know about loyalty, patience, and compassion." He paused, swallowing hard against the lump in his throat. "He loved his family deeply, and he always put us first, even when it meant sacrificing his own happiness."

Jobe clenched his fists, trying to summon the strength to continue. In his mind, he saw his father's face—strong, kind, and wise. A man who had lost so much yet still managed to carry on with grace and dignity.

"Even after my brother…passed away, he never let go of his faith. And now, I must find a way to do the same."

Jobe's voice wavered, and he wiped his eyes with the back of his hand. "I will honor my father's memory by living as he did—with courage, integrity, and love."

The wind seemed to pause for a moment as if granting Jobe the silence he needed to finish. "Goodbye, Dad," he whispered hoarsely. "You were my rock, my hero, and my guiding light. I hope I can make you proud."

Jobe gazed at his father's casket, struggling to comprehend the enormity of his loss. He felt Jonathan's presence beside him, offering silent support, but it was little comfort against the crushing weight of his grief.

The rain began to fall, each drop a cold reminder of the emptiness that filled Jobe. A single question echoed through Jobe's mind: What now?

THE OMINOUS CLOUDS above the cemetery mirrored the heaviness in Delilah's gut as she approached Jobe, who stood alone by his father's grave. The wind picked up, sending dead leaves dancing around them like restless souls. A shiver ran down Delilah's spine as cold raindrops fell into her crimson hair.

She could feel Jobe's pain, almost a physical force that seemed to drain away all the air around them. She wanted to step forward and offer him her comfort, but she didn't know what to say.

Delilah shifted uncertainly on her feet, biting her lip as she tried to gather her thoughts. As much as she wanted to come up with the perfect words of comfort, all she could think of was that there were no words that could ever fill the void left by Jobe's father's death.

But then again, maybe all Jobe needed was a little bit of understanding and compassion—something Delilah knew she could provide. Taking a deep breath, Delilah stepped forward until she was standing right beside Jobe. He glanced at her briefly before looking away again, his grief palpable.

"Jobe," she whispered, placing a hand on his shoulder, feeling his tense muscles beneath her fingers. "I'm so sorry."

"Thanks, Delilah." His voice cracked with emotion. "I can't believe he's gone."

"Neither can I," she admitted, her thoughts drifting to her own broken relationship with Abe. She knew all too well the pain of losing someone you love, even if they were still alive.

Delilah looked at the other mourners gathered near the gravesite, their faces solemn and tear-streaked. The pastor opened his Bible, and his deep voice resonated through the air, offering words of comfort and prayers for the deceased. As the service progressed, Delilah found herself grieving not only for Jobe's father but also for the shattered bond between her and her own dad.

"Didn't think this would be happening so soon," said Jobe, his eyes never leaving the casket.

"I know," Delilah choked out, her vision blurred by tears. "But life is cruel like that."

"Yes. Yes, it is," said Jobe, his tone overwhelmingly bitter.

As the pastor finished the final prayer, the pallbearers stepped forward to lower the casket into the earth. Delilah felt Jobe's grip on her hand tighten, his knuckles turning white. She squeezed back, trying to offer him some small measure of support.

Delilah didn't know how to make Jobe feel better, but what she did know was that she would be there for him. She couldn't undo the pain and sorrow he was feeling, but she could provide a listening ear and a shoulder to cry on when he needed it. She would stay by his side through this journey of healing and grief, no matter how long it took.

As the mourners began to disperse, Delilah noticed two men lingering near the edge of the cemetery. Their hushed voices carried on the wind, and she caught snippets of their conversation.

"...suspicious figure... construction site... day of the accident..."

Her mind buzzed as she realized they might be discussing something related to Jobe's father's death. She glanced at Jobe, wondering if he had heard them too, but he was lost in his grief, oblivious to the world.

Unable to resist the pull of her feelings any longer, Delilah took Jobe's hand in hers.

"Jobe," she whispered, her voice cracking with emotion, "you're not alone in this."

He looked up, his eyes red-rimmed and filled with pain. As their gazes locked, a surge of connection and understanding passed between them.

"Delilah, I—" Jobe started, his voice choking with tears.

"Shh." She stepped closer and placed a gentle hand on his arm. "We don't have to say anything."

For a moment, they stood there in silence, allowing their shared sorrow to bind them together. Their fingers intertwined with an unspoken promise of support and companionship.

"Remember when our dads used to take us fishing?" Delilah asked softly, a bittersweet smile tugging at her lips as memories of happier times flooded her mind.

Jobe nodded, his grip tightening on her hand. "Yeah, they'd always compete to see who could catch the biggest fish. Your dad usually won, if I remember correctly."

"Only because my mom would secretly help him," she confessed, laughter bubbling up despite the heaviness in her chest. "She'd throw little pieces of worms in the water where my dad cast his line to attract more fish. They thought we didn't know, but we were always watching them."

"Your parents had something special," Jobe said, his voice laced with a sadness that Delilah wished he didn't have to endure. "I always admired how much they loved each other."

"And your father was amazing," she replied earnestly, squeezing his hand in reassurance. "He was so proud of you, Jobe. Don't ever forget that."

Delilah noticed a renewed sense of purpose stirring within her. Their grief had brought them closer, but it wouldn't define them forever.

As they stood there, their hands clasped tightly, Delilah knew that their journey would be filled with many challenges. But with Jobe by her side and the connection they shared blossoming like a beacon in the darkness, she was ready to face whatever lay ahead.

While the rain had been coming down gently at first, it quickly grew in intensity. Delilah wished the drops could wash away the sadness that hung heavy in the air. The rain fell in waves, drenching Jobe and Delilah as they stood near the graveside. Delilah ached with empathy for Jobe's grief, just as it ached as she considered the strained relationship with her own father.

Delilah looked around. Most of the guests had left but for a few stragglers, and Jobe still stood by his father's grave, motionless, looking down with a miserable gaze. Rain fell freely down upon them, and a large tree stood not far from Delilah on the right, its leafless branches twisted and gnarled. The tree was dying, Delilah saw, looking dry and cracked and thirsty. It hadn't rained in a good while, and Delilah wondered if the current rainfall would be enough to bring the tree back to life.

Rain was a tricky thing. Too little, and things died, she considered as she looked at the dying tree. Too much—and she glanced west toward the Gozan River—and it could cause a flood. It was something that needed to be balanced. She wondered, glancing over at Jobe, if Jobe would be able to come to terms with his loss and bring balance back into his life. She wondered if she could find that balance with her own father as well.

Delilah looked back at the tree. She saw the struggle it had endured to stay alive, and as she watched it sway in the wind, its few dying leaves swept off its branches and fluttered down to the ground. Her eyes filled with tears for both herself and Jobe. As she kept gazing at it, Delilah thought of her dying relationship with her father.

Then Delilah noticed the mysterious figure she had overheard earlier. His face was partially obscured by the brim of his hat, and he was talking to one of the only other guests who remained. There was something unnerving about him, but she couldn't pinpoint it.

Delilah slipped away from Jobe and edged closer to the stranger. As she approached, she overheard him talking to the man next to him in hushed tones.

"I know what I saw," the man said eerily. "There was definitely someone snooping around the construction site on the day of the accident. He was wearing a backpack, and he went right up to that scaffold—the same one Hosea fell from."

Really?" the other man replied, visibly shaken. "Doesn't anyone else know? "

The first man sighed. "I don't think so. But I didn't think it was something I should keep to myself."

Delilah's mind reeling with possibilities. Was there more to Jobe's father's death than a simple accident? She gazed at the mysterious figure, who now seemed to be eyeing her with curiosity.

"Who are you?" she asked boldly, taking a few more steps toward him.

The man hesitated before answering, his voice low and gravelly. "Just a concerned friend," he replied, not quite meeting her gaze. "Someone who wants to see justice served for Hosea."

Delilah studied him, her adrenaline rushing. His face was a blur under the brim of his hat, and she could feel the mystery surrounding him. She had no way of knowing who this man was or what he wanted with Jobe's father's death, but one thing was clear—he knew more about Hosea Johnson's death than everyone else around them.

"Justice?" Delilah echoed, her suspicions growing. "He fell from a scaffold."

"I'm not denying that," the mystery man hissed. "But the question is why."

Delilah's stomach lurched, and a lump formed in her throat. Was it possible that there was something sinister involved? She inhaled deeply, her mind spinning with so many questions. She knew she had to find out the truth—for Jobe's sake.

She looked up at the man, her voice quiet but determined. "What do you know?"

"More than anyone else," he answered cryptically. "Somebody tampered with that scaffold," he said, glancing over to where Jobe stood alone. Without another word, he turned on his heel and walked away.

Delilah was frozen in shock, her mind swimming with all the possibilities that were now unfolding before her. She thought of Jobe and all the pain he had had to go through since his father's death.

If Jobe's dad's death wasn't an accident, then Jobe needs to know that.

Delilah had to find out what really happened to Jobe's dad—no matter the cost. She was determined to uncover the truth, even if it meant going up against a powerful force that wanted to keep it hidden.

As the funeral came to an end, Delilah couldn't shake the feeling that they were on the cusp of discovering something terrible—a secret that threatened to shatter the fragile peace they'd found in their shared grief. As Jobe approached her, his face pale and drawn, she decided to keep her newfound knowledge to herself for the time being.

She was sure that telling him his dad's death might not have been an accident would only bring more pain and suffering. Until she had proof, she wouldn't say anything. She would let him grieve because that's what he needed right now.

But Delilah also knew that the truth would come out eventually, and when it did, she wouldn't back down from uncovering it—for Jobe's sake.

But as they walked away from the graveside, hand in hand, Delilah glanced back at the spot where the mysterious figure had stood. Who was he? What did he know? And how much danger were they all in?

CHAPTER 3

Abe stood at the window, watching the sunset paint the sky in vibrant oranges and reds. The beauty of the moment did little to ease the heaviness in his chest. He thought about Jobe, who had lost his father, and prayed he was coping with the grief. The tragedy reminded Abe of life's fleeting nature—one moment here, the next gone, like the setting sun. This realization made him yearn for a more peaceful relationship with his daughter, Delilah.

"Time is short," he mumbled to himself, eyes still fixed on the horizon.

Time was short, and he couldn't bear the thought of leaving this world with their relationship strained as it was. Abe knew he needed to make amends, and fast.

He recalled the harshness in his voice when he told Delilah she should quit her job at Alexandria Meat. A pang of guilt rippled through him. His daughter was passionate about her work, and he'd dismissed her devotion so casually. Abe decided he would make dinner for Delilah as a peace offering.

"Delilah!" he called. "I'm making dinner tonight! Join me?"

"Sure, Dad," she replied, her voice cautious. It hurt Abe to hear the wariness in her tone.

Abe set about to prepare a meal, humming as he chopped vegetables, the sound of his knife slicing through the carrots and onions and creating a comforting rhythm. He welcomed the familiarity of it—the way it reminded him of hours spent in the kitchen with his mother many years ago. A soft smile graced his face as he added garlic and herbs to the pan and inhaled deeply. The aroma of simmering stew filled the room, bringing warmth and comfort.

He opened a bottle of wine and poured two glasses, one for himself and one for Delilah. Placing them on the table, he went back to finish making dinner. When everything was ready, Abe called out to Delilah.

"Come on in! Dinner's ready."

The pair sat down at the table and shared stories about their day over dinner. It was so good to reconnect after a long time of not seeing eye to eye, and Abe couldn't remember the last time they had eaten dinner together.

But as they continued their meal, the tension between them remained palpable. Abe tried to steer the conversation toward lighter topics, but their differences over Alexandria Meat were unavoidable.

"Delilah, I understand your concern for the workers," Abe said, trying to keep his tone gentle. "But we need the company to be more profitable. It's our livelihood."

"Isn't there a way to do that without sacrificing the well-being of the people who work for us?" Delilah shot back, her eyes blazing with conviction.

"Sometimes sacrifices have to be made," Abe replied, masking his frustration. "You can't make everyone happy, Delilah."

"Maybe not," Delilah retorted, her voice strained. She nervously twisted her red hair around one of her fingers. "But at least I can try."

The silence that followed illuminated the abyss between them. Abe knew his words had driven a deeper wedge into their already fractured relationship, and he wished he didn't have to discuss these matters with his daughter. But they worked at the same company, and they were family. It was unavoidable.

Abe ached for Delilah, and he yearned to find a way to bridge the gap.

"Delilah, I love you," Abe said, his voice wavering. "But we need to find a way to make this work."

Gritting his teeth, Abe clenched the edge of the table. He stared at the worn wood, ingrained with years of memories, and tried to find the right words. But deep down, he knew he couldn't compromise his need for Alexandria Meat to remain profitable. The company's survival was vital, not only for him, but for Delilah as well. He wouldn't let her throw it all away.

"Delilah," he began, his voice tight with suppressed emotion, "I know you care about the workers, but we must focus on keeping the business alive. We can't help anyone if we go under."

The tense silence that followed was broken only by the ticking of the clock on the wall, each second a reminder of their dwindling time to find a solution. It weighed heavily on Abe, the pressure building in his chest like an approaching storm.

As Abe looked at his daughter, his thoughts were a whirlwind, a maelstrom of emotions he struggled to navigate. He loved his daughter more than anything, but he also felt that she was young and naïve, oblivious to the harsh realities of the world. She didn't realize that his way was the best way, even if she didn't understand why. Then he stopped a moment to ponder that thought. Was that even true? *Is my way really the best way?*

Abe thought about every time Delilah had come to him for advice, recalling the numerous challenges she'd faced throughout her life, both personal and professional. Each one left its mark on her, shaping her into the woman she was today—strong, determined, yet vulnerable to her own expectations.

I hope she's not being too hard on herself.

"Can't we find a balance?" Delilah implored, her voice cracking with desperation. "A way to make the company viable while still taking care of our people?"

Her pleading tone broke Abe's heart. She was trying so hard to compromise—and so was he—trying as hard as he could.

"I hope we can, Delilah," Abe said earnestly. "I hope we can."

"Well, can we start with a raise for the workers?" Delilah asked. "You know they deserve it."

Abe's mind was blown, and his mouth fell nearly all the way down to the dining room table. "A raise for everyone? That's the last thing we need!"

"It's what *they* need," Delilah said pointedly.

"It's what we all need!" Abe snapped, his frustration starting to get the best of him. "But not all of us are going to get one. Nothing is ever that simple. You have to make tough decisions sometimes, ones that might hurt in the short term but benefit everyone in the long run."

"Is that what you believe?" Delilah asked, and Abe heard pain, and maybe even a bit of anger, in her voice. "Or is that what you tell yourself to justify your actions?"

"Enough!" Abe slammed his fist on the table, causing Delilah to flinch. The sudden outburst left them both stunned, staring at each other with a mixture of anger and disbelief. *I can't believe I did that.*

Delilah looked at him like a stranger, the shock from his eruption painfully clear in her eyes. He wanted to make her this dinner to bring them closer, to destroy the growing edge between them. It was evident, however, that he had done quite the opposite.

"What's gotten into you, Dad?" she asked with venom in her voice.

"What's gotten into me?" Abe questioned, angry all over again. "I'm trying to keep a company afloat and to pay for a house and all its bills! Something you obviously don't know anything about!"

Delilah sprang up from her chair. "I'm not going to sit here while you yell and hit the table! And I'm not taking your side when you don't care about people's jobs!"

"Oh yeah?" Abe yelled.

"Yeah!" Delilah yelled back. "And I'm not staying in this house either! I'm packing my stuff and leaving!" And she stormed off to her room.

"Yeah, why don't you go ahead and do that!" Abe yelled. "Sounds good to me!"

WHAT AM I supposed to do without my father?

Jobe sank back into his bed sheets, his body enveloped in a thick miasma of despair. He had been sleeping most of the day, trying to avoid thoughts of his father's death. But as tears streamed down his face, he realized that he couldn't escape this pain no matter how hard he tried. It felt surreal—a bad dream he couldn't wake up from.

CHAPTER 3

But the worst part of it was that it wasn't a dream at all. It was real life. His life, however new and surprising.

The reality of his situation was too much for Jobe to bear: His father was gone, and there was nothing he could do about it. Jobe buried his face in the pillow and let out a loud sob, feeling his heart was being ripped out with each breath. The air seemed heavy and oppressive, pressing down on him like an invisible weight as if to remind him that life would never be the same again.

He lay there in silence in a timeless void until, eventually exhaustion set in, and he drifted off to sleep yet again.

In his dreams, he was transported to a different time when things were much simpler. He and his father were walking along the beach, laughing and talking about what they wanted to do with their lives. Jobe felt the sun on his skin and heard the waves lapping against the shore. His father looked so peaceful, as if nothing in the world could ever touch him.

As they continued walking, Jobe's father stopped and told him that he was proud of him—that he had grown into an amazing young man who could achieve anything that he set his sights on. Jobe felt a million stars were burning inside of him as his father embraced him tightly.

Then Jobe woke up, reality hitting him fast and hard. His father was gone forever, and no amount of dreaming would bring him back. Tears filled Jobe's eyes as he realized that all those beautiful memories would never be experienced again.

Amid his turmoil, Jobe managed a moment of self-reflection. *How am I feeling?* he considered. The answer came quickly, the grimness of it squeezing his soul and threatening to snuff out its light. *I feel I can't do this without him. I feel I can't go on.*

Eventually, Jobe mustered the strength to get up and walk into the bathroom. His vision was still blurred from all the tears he had shed, but he could make out his reflection in the mirror—a figure that was no longer recognizable after everything that had happened. Anger burned within him, and he grabbed the collar of his t-shirt with both hands, gripping it tightly.

He's never coming back! More tears rushed down from his eyes. *He's never coming back!*

Jobe's fists tightened, his hands pulling down and apart, his T-shirt ripping under his rage. Seams popped, and the shirt tore apart, and Jobe yelled in anguish, as angry and helpless as he'd ever been.

He slowly sank onto the cold tile floor, burying his face in his hands as silent sobs shook his body.

A COLD EMPTINESS gripped Delilah as she marched to her room and began packing a suitcase. The night had been a disaster, and now there was something broken between them that could never be fixed. As she shoved clothes and other essentials into her suitcase, Delilah's heart cracked in two.

It felt as though the air had been drained from the world, leaving a void of despair in its place. Delilah was numb, as if all emotion had left her body and there was nothing she could do to bring it back. She wanted to call out to him, to apologize for whatever part she may have played in his outburst and make things right again—but no words would come out. It was like she had lost the ability to speak entirely, leaving only an unbearable silence in its wake.

Delilah thought of special memories she had of her dad. She remembered when he had taken her fishing at the Gozan River, where she could feel the warm sun on her skin and hear the gentle flow of water as it cascaded along its banks, his strong arms guiding hers as he taught her how to cast a line, his patient voice giving her instructions on how to reel in her catch.

She recalled the time when he had shown her how to swim, supporting her with a firm hand under each arm just beneath the surface of the lake. She felt like she was flying as she kicked and paddled through the clear blue water, laughing with joy and excitement at being able to move so freely.

Delilah smiled through newly made tears as these fond memories flashed before her—memories that were more precious now than ever before.

She thought again about apologizing, but then her father's shouts echoed in her mind, his anger, his hurtful words. First, he had suggested she shouldn't work at Alexandria Meat anymore. And tonight, he had slammed his fist on the table and frightened her. When she said she was leaving, he had shouted at her that she should. The anger and disrespect he had shown her was just too much, and that, taken with his disregard for the employees...no, she wouldn't live under his roof anymore. She continued to pack her suitcase until she felt she had everything she needed to live away from the house, and then she got into her car and drove to the nearest hotel.

But as Delilah unpacked her suitcase in her hotel room, all she thought about was that her father was gone from her life. *Why am I acting like he's dead or something?* And it struck Delilah that their relationship was so far gone that she had essentially lost him completely. *Like Jobe,* she thought sadly, feeling grief for both Jobe and herself. They had both lost their fathers, in a way. The only difference was that she had a chance to get hers back.

But how? Delilah wondered, but only for a moment. *Alexandria Meat, that's how.*

If she could save the family business, then maybe it would give her and her father some common ground to stand on once again. A way to repair their relationship and give them their foundation back. There was a rush of adrenaline as determination filled her chest, but with it came a wave of fear—fear of failure, fear that their relationship wouldn't be mended even if she did succeed. The pressure was overwhelming, and Delilah closed her eyes and breathed in deeply.

If someone didn't act soon, the plant might close down, leaving hundreds unemployed and the town without its primary source of income. *If the workers aren't treated right, they'll go on strike, and production will come to a halt.*

Delilah pondered further, knowing that, conversely, if management didn't find a way to make the company more profitable, they'd start laying people off. Either way, the plant was in danger of going under.

But the thought of taking on the responsibility filled her with dread.

Her mind raced as she weighed the pros and cons, the stakes higher than ever before. It felt as if she was standing on the edge of a cliff, one wrong move away from plummeting into an abyss. The fear of failure gripped her like a vice, making it difficult to breathe.

I can't let my anxiety get the best of me, Delilah thought, clenching her fists. *But is this something I really want to take on?*

Was she capable of saving the plant and preserving her father's legacy? Or would her fear of not being successful doom them all to ruin?

Her thoughts spiraled, the fear of failure looming large in her mind.

This is not my area of expertise, she thought. *If I try to help, I'll probably only make things worse between us.*

No, trying to save the plant wasn't a good idea at all. While she had made her decision, she didn't exactly feel good about it, so she got out her journal and began to write an entry:

I don't want to get involved with trying to save the plant. My father and I are so far removed from each other that I'm afraid that taking on this job will only make things worse between us. I feel overwhelmed and intimidated by the task of saving something so important—not only for our town but for my dad's legacy as well. It's too big of a risk for me to take. It crushes me to know there's nothing I can do, but for now, all I can do is hope...hope that someone else comes along and finds a way to keep Alexandria Meat alive.

Just then, Delilah remembered that her best friend, Michelle, was supposed to be back in town soon. *She might even be here already, even though I haven't heard from her yet.*

She could think of no better way to clear her mind and even get some advice than to go see her. It was better than sitting alone at night in an empty hotel room.

So Delilah got in her car and drove to Michelle's house, anxious as she stood at her friend's doorstep and knocked on the door.

The porch light turned on, and then the door flew open swiftly. "Delilah!" Michelle practically shouted.

"Hey, Michelle!" Delilah hugged her best friend. "I wasn't sure if you had made it home yet."

"Yeah! I've been back for about a week or so," said Michelle, pulling Delilah in from the night. "I just opened a bottle of wine, and you're going to drink it with me."

Michelle ran off into the kitchen as Delilah sat down on the couch.

"Fine, I guess," Delilah teased as Michelle returned with a bottle of wine and two glasses.

"So what's new?" Michelle asked as she poured them both a glass.

"Well, I left home," said Delilah. She swirled her wine and took a sip.

"Great!" said Michelle, scooting close to her on the couch. "You have your own place here in town?"

Delilah sighed. "Not exactly. Dad and I aren't talking," she confessed.

Michelle's jaw dropped. "You're not talking? What do you mean? Why?"

"It's Alexandria Meat," said Delilah, shaking her head at everything that had happened. "There have been issues between the workers and management. The workers want better treatment, and management wants more efficient production metrics. And I was caught in the middle, and it felt like I had to choose sides." Delilah tugged on one of her crimson pigtails. "My father agrees with management and thinks we need higher production numbers. But I know everyone is working hard. Maybe even too hard. Long days, little pay; they really deserve more."

Michelle breathed in deep, taking it all in. "No way," she said.

"I don't know what's gotten into him," said Delilah with a shrug, "but I can't be around him."

"You two have always had an excellent relationship," said Michelle. She shook her head like she couldn't believe what Delilah had told her.

"I know. That's why it hurts so much."

"But you guys will make up, right?" Michelle offered, her voice hopeful. "You'll go back home soon."

Delilah shook her head. "No. I don't think so."

CHAPTER 4

Jobe tossed and turned as he tried to fall asleep. Every night since his father passed had been this way. He'd doze off and immediately start dreaming about his father. In his dreams, things were the way they were before. His father was still alive, and nothing had changed. But suddenly, in a moment of lucidity, he'd realize the dream wasn't real, and he'd awake with a start. And then he'd cry at his new reality.

When he did finally get to sleep, the morning came like a cruel reminder that he would have to endure yet another day without his dad.

He got up and moseyed around the house. He fed Smokey and took him for a walk, and he realized when he got back that he had forgotten to eat himself. He had no appetite.

He went all the way until dinner time before he finally made himself a meager sandwich. Even still, he ate it because he knew he needed to. Not because he wanted to.

He couldn't imagine a time when food would taste good again. When the hole in his life would be filled. When the world would seem normal again.

PATH BLOCKED

5

THE FIRST LIGHT of dawn seeped through the hotel room's curtains, casting a warm glow over Delilah's face as she stirred in her sleep. Her eyes fluttered open, and she found herself staring at the ceiling, her thoughts immediately consumed by the mysterious man she had approached at the funeral.

"Somebody tampered with that scaffold," he had said, his voice gravelly and cold. She shivered at the memory, recalling the chilling statement. His scent—cigarette smoke and something metallic—still lingered in her nostrils as if he were standing right beside her.

With a determined sigh, Delilah swung her legs out of bed and pulled on her clothes. She owed it to Jobe to find out more about his father's death, and the construction site seemed like the best place to start.

As she approached the site, her chest pounded louder than war drums. The high scaffold towered above her like a dark omen, and she could picture Jobe's dad plummeting to the unforgiving ground below. She imagined the rush of wind past his ears, the terror that must have filled his eyes as he realized there was nothing to break his fall.

Delilah clenched her fists and steeled herself, knowing that she had to climb up there to uncover what had really happened. She glanced around the empty construction site, confident no one was watching, and then she grabbed hold of the first rung of the ladder that led upward.

Her palms grew sweaty, her grip slipping slightly as she ascended higher and higher. The world below became a blur of colors and shapes, and she could feel the wind tugging at her hair, threatening to tear her away from the precarious scaffold.

"Come on, Delilah," she whispered to herself, her breaths coming in short gasps. "You can do this. For Jobe."

Finally, she reached the top of the scaffold. She took a moment to steady herself, her thoughts spinning with questions. What if the man at the funeral was right? What would she find up here that could shed light on the tragedy that had befallen Jobe's family?

As she looked around the sprawling construction site below, Delilah knew without a doubt that she would stop at nothing to uncover the truth, no matter how dangerous or painful it might be. A new, chilling question began to form in her mind: who else wanted the truth to stay hidden?

Delilah shifted to her hands and knees for balance, knowing that what had happened to Jobe's dad could very well happen to her as well.

The metallic clang of the shifting scaffold and the whistling wind were her only companions as Delilah crawled across the platform atop the high scaffold. Her eyes widened in disbelief when she noticed the slick, dark substance covering the surface.

"Oil?" Delilah muttered, feeling its slippery texture between her fingers. She suddenly realized how treacherous her situation was—especially if she was standing upright—one misstep could send her plummeting to the ground below. The cold breeze whipped around her, causing her to shiver.

"Focus," she whispered, steadying herself on her hands and knees. She cautiously continued forward, her muscles tensing with each calculated movement. She no longer felt the thrill of adventure or the sense of satisfaction that came from uncovering hidden truths; instead, fear gripped her like a vice, making it difficult to breathe.

As she slid and scrambled over the oil-slicked platform, her thoughts tumbled about: Who had put the oil here? Was it an accident or something far more sinister? And most importantly, should she tell Jobe about this discovery?

She didn't want to trouble Jobe further, who was already in anguish over his loss, if it turned out to be just a coincidence. No, she would only bring it up if she had more concrete details, something more incriminating. She would, however, tell the police. She wouldn't be able to bear it if there had been wrongdoing involved and justice wasn't served because she had withheld information.

She carefully retraced her steps, inching back toward the ladder that would lead her to solid ground. Each rung seemed to mock her, reminding her of the danger she had just faced. When she finally reached the bottom, she gulped in a lungful of air, feeling both relieved and unsettled.

CHAPTER 4

She went right to the police station, telling them about the oil she found on the scaffold and what the man at the funeral had told her. They logged the details, thanking her for the information.

"We have no reason to believe foul play is involved," a detective told her. "At least not yet. But if that changes, this is good information to have."

She left the police station and went back to her hotel room, getting out her hair curler and going into the bathroom. A new hairstyle always seemed to bring her back to life, and the experience she had just had at the construction site had been harrowing.

Delilah stood before the mirror, clenching locks of her crimson hair between the curler's grip. She knew she had to do something, but she didn't know what. Even if the oil was a coincidence, Jobe still deserved to know. So after she had styled all of her tresses into big, looping curls, she got into her car and drove to Jobe's house.

As she walked towards Jobe's house, her mind swirled with unanswered questions and unspoken fears. The sunset cast a fiery glow over the city, a fitting backdrop for the storm brewing inside her.

She knocked on the door, and Jobe opened it a few moments later and invited her in.

"Jobe," Delilah said, her voice cracking as she stepped into his living room. "I... I have something to tell you."

"Hey, Delilah, what's up?" Jobe asked, his eyes filled with concern as he leaned against the wall, Smokey, his loyal puppy, wagging its tail by his side.

Delilah sank into the couch, the weight of her words pressing down on her chest. But Delilah just couldn't bring herself to tell him about the oil. "I…I'm no longer speaking with my father." Her voice cracked, betraying her façade of strength.

"Your father? What happened?" Jobe questioned, his brow furrowed.

It was incredible to Delilah how much empathy Jobe showed, especially with what he was going through.

"Alexandria Meat," she whispered, unable to look Jobe in the eye. "We fought badly about it. The workers are being treated so unfairly, and he just doesn't care."

"Delilah…" Jobe said. "I'm so sorry to hear that."

Silence stretched between them, tension winding like a coil, ready to snap. Smokey nudged Delilah's hand, sensing her distress and offering solace in his own way. She returned the gesture, stroking his soft fur as if it could somehow soothe the ache.

"Come here," Jobe said softly, opening his arms for her. Delilah hesitated, then succumbed to the desperate need for comfort. They hugged each other tightly, both mourning the loss of their fathers in different ways—one to death, the other to irreconcilable differences.

As they held each other close, Delilah's thoughts sank. How could her father, a man she had always looked up to, be so blind to the injustice within his own company? She knew the fight had changed their relationship forever, and yet she couldn't bring herself to regret standing up for what she believed in.

At that moment, Delilah realized the true cost of following her convictions, but it was a price she was willing to pay. The sun had set on her old life, and as darkness enveloped them, she found a new sense of resolve in Jobe's embrace. Together, they would face whatever challenges lay ahead, even if it meant leaving behind those they once held dear.

"Jobe," Delilah began, taking a deep breath, "I went to the construction site today, and—"

"The construction site?" Jobe asked, his voice trembling. "What about it?"

CHAPTER 5

Jobe thought it strange that Delilah had mentioned the construction site yesterday, and the way she had brought it up made it seem like she had uncovered something important. But instead, all she had said was, "It made me think of your father. I miss him."

I miss him too.

The sun glared down on him as he stood on the edge of the open field, the tall grass swaying in the breeze. He was heavy with grief, each labored breath a reminder of his father's absence. He stared at the small yellow tennis ball in his hand, lost in thought. It felt like a lifetime ago when his dad had taught him to play catch, his strong hands guiding Jobe's small ones, showing him how to grip the ball just right.

"All right, Smokey, let's do this," he muttered, wiping away tears. The golden retriever puppy wagged his tail, his eyes bright with anticipation. With a deep breath, Jobe hurled the ball into the distance, watching as it arched through the air.

"Fetch!" he yelled, his voice cracking. Smokey bolted after the ball, running through the grass with boundless energy. As he watched the pup disappear into the field, Jobe clenched his fists.

"I hate that church," he whispered, bitterness seeping into his words. The construction site was still fresh in his memory, that half-built abominable building, the high scaffold his father had fallen from—it gnawed at him relentlessly. How could a holy place like a church be responsible for his father's death?

Smokey returned triumphantly, the slobbery ball clutched between his teeth. Jobe forced a smile and patted the enthusiastic pup on the head. "Good boy." He wouldn't let his emotions get the best of him; he needed to focus on what was here and now—his responsibilities, like taking care of Smokey.

In the weeks since his father's death, Jobe had found solace in his new companion. Smokey's boundless energy and enthusiasm for life was something he needed right now. Even on days when grief threatened to consume him, Jobe had found himself getting into a routine: playing with Smokey, taking him for long walks around the neighborhood, and teaching him new tricks. It was like his dad was still there, watching from afar with that slight smirk of pride on his face.

Jobe never missed an opportunity to play catch with Smokey, and it seemed to be helping him cope with the grief. Each time he threw the ball into the distance, he was throwing away his worries and fears—however temporarily—into oblivion. His dad used to love throwing balls around with Smokey too, so it felt like a link between them.

Maybe that's all I need, Jobe thought hopefully. *To grieve my own way.*

Later that day, Jobe found himself in the small back yard behind his house, attempting to teach Smokey to sit. The sun had dipped lower in the sky by now, casting long shadows across the ground. "Sit, Smokey," he commanded, his voice firm and steady. The puppy cocked his head to one side, staring up at Jobe with wide, innocent eyes but not making any attempt to sit.

Jobe gently pushed down on the puppy's butt, but Smokey didn't budge. "Come on, Smokey," Jobe pleaded, growing more frustrated by the second. "You just don't want to learn your lessons today, do you?" He sank down onto the grass, feeling more than a little defeated. As he stared at the stubborn pup, he pondered over the lessons he had learned from his father. What wisdom had been passed down to him that would guide him through this turbulent time?

As Jobe sat in the cool grass, his thoughts swirling, he felt an overwhelming sense of loss. His father's influence had shaped so much of who he was, from his career as a firefighter to his love for early mornings. Now, all he had left were memories and unanswered questions.

"Maybe it's not only about the lessons we're taught," Jobe whispered to himself, looking into Smokey's trusting eyes. "Maybe it's about how we choose to carry them forward." With renewed determination, Jobe stood up and faced the golden retriever once more.

"All right, Smokey. Let's try this again."

Jobe worked with Smokey a bit longer, trying several times to get the puppy to sit and only succeeding once. And that was good enough for Jobe. They headed back home and didn't play again together until the evening.

When it was time for Smokey's evening walk, Jobe took the puppy out again and walked through the town, Smokey bounding along beside him. As they passed O'Malley's Pub, he caught a glimpse of Delilah and Michelle through the window, talking animatedly and laughing together. For a moment, Jobe's chest ached, and he longed for that easy companionship.

"Maybe I need the support of my friends," he said out loud, thinking about his best friend Jonathan. "Maybe that's another way to grieve my own way." Smokey looked up at him, his tail wagging as if to agree. With one last glance through the window at Delilah, Jobe continued on his way, each step carrying the tension of unresolved emotions.

Later that evening, Jobe sat on his porch with Smokey curled up beside him. His father had always taught him to take action, and since it had occurred to Jobe that he must find ways to grieve in his own way, his priority would be doing just that.

Time with Smokey was one thing that definitely helped, and the next thing he would try was time with his friends: Jonathan—and even Delilah.

As the last light of day faded, Jobe felt a renewed sense of purpose. There were still many unanswered questions in his life, but he knew he wouldn't face them alone. With the support of his friends, he would forge ahead, determined to honor his father's memory and make a difference in the world around him.

As the stars began to twinkle in the night sky, a sense of anticipation hung in the air, hinting at the challenges and adventures that lay ahead.

THE CRACKLING LAUGHTER of Delilah and Michelle was abruptly interrupted by the sound of a fiddle striking its first high note. The sudden music seemed to sweep through O'Malley's, enveloping the pub in a lively Irish melody. Delilah glanced around, her eyes sparkling with curiosity as she watched patrons tap their feet and sway to the rhythm.

"Delilah," Michelle asked, leaning in closer to be heard over the music, "what's been on your mind lately? You've got that faraway look again." Her voice was warm and caring, like a comforting embrace.

Delilah hesitated for a moment, her gaze drifting toward the window where Jobe had just passed by. "I miss my dad," she admitted, her voice barely audible above the fiddle's tune. "I'm not used to not having him in my life."

Michelle's expression softened, her fingers reaching out to gently squeeze Delilah's hand. "I know this must be really hard. I know how close you two were."

Delilah sighed and squeezed her friend's hand. "It's like we're dead to each other. Like he doesn't even exist anymore. I honestly don't even know how to deal with it."

"Deal with it your way," Michelle said simply.

"My way?" Delilah questioned.

Michelle nodded. "Yeah. What do you think would help? What would make you feel better?"

Delilah bit her lip. "Well, I've been thinking about this a lot, and if something doesn't change, the plant will likely go under. And that would crush my dad. We need the workers to be happy and have higher production output. But how the heck can we have both?"

"That's the challenge," Michelle said knowingly. "A challenge I know you can figure out."

"Save the plant for Dad," Delilah mused aloud. "That's what I would do if it were up to me."

Michelle grinned at her. "It is up to you. You got this, hon."

Feeling encouraged by Michelle's unwavering faith in her abilities, Delilah felt more determined than ever. "You're right," she said, her voice more robust now. "I think I might be up to the challenge after all."

As the fiddle's tune reached its crescendo, Delilah felt invigorated by the passionate music.

"Let's toast to that," Michelle suggested, raising her glass. Delilah followed suit, their glasses clinking in a symphony of hope and friendship.

"Challenge accepted." Delilah chuckled, her thoughts dancing with unanswered questions and newfound resolve.

The clink of their glasses called keenly through the air. She inhaled long and slow, feeling the rich aroma of O'Malley's dark wood and earthy ale mingle with the scent of Michelle's jasmine perfume.

Delilah beamed, realizing that she was lucky to have a wonderful friend like Michelle. One who was always there for her and willing to lend an ear when needed. Knowing that she could always rely on Michelle's wise words of encouragement made Delilah feel more confident in her decision.

The bond between them was strong, fortified by years of mutual trust and understanding. This friendship had undoubtedly become one of Delilah's most treasured possessions—a source of joy that never failed to bring a smile to even the gloomiest days. In Michelle, she'd found someone who truly understood her struggles and believed in her potential—without judgment or expectation.

"Michelle, I really appreciate your support through all of this," she said, her voice thick with emotion. "I don't know what I'd do without you."

"Hey, that's what friends are for," Michelle replied, squeezing Delilah's hand. "We'll figure it out. Delilah, remember that no matter the outcome, I'll always be here for you," Michelle said, her voice steady and confident.

Delilah looked into her friend's eyes, searching for the support she desperately needed to face the enormity of saving Alexandria Meat. "Thank you, Michelle. I just don't know if I can do it," Delilah admitted, her fingers nervously tracing the rim of her coffee mug.

"Of course, you can," Michelle insisted, leaning in closer. "You're stronger than you give yourself credit for."

The atmosphere of O'Malley's wrapped around them like a warm embrace, offering a temporary reprieve from the cold reality outside. The smell of freshly brewed coffee intermingled with the faint scent of aged wood and hearty Irish stew, creating a sense of comfort and familiarity that Delilah cherished in moments like these.

As they spoke, the lively sound of live Irish music played by a fiddler and a guitarist filled the air, their upbeat melodies lifting the spirits of the pub's patrons. Delilah couldn't help but tap her foot along to the rhythm, momentarily forgetting her troubles as she lost herself in the music.

"Michelle, how did you find the strength to follow your dreams?" Delilah asked, her eyes locked on her friend's.

"By realizing that regret is far heavier than fear," Michelle replied, her words punctuated by the crescendo of the fiddle. "Life is full of uncertainties, Delilah. But taking chances, making mistakes, and learning from them—that's where true growth comes from."

Delilah took a deep breath, her chest tightening as she processed Michelle's advice. She knew her friend was right, but the thought of facing the unknown still terrified her.

"Can I truly save Alexandria Meat without losing myself in the process? How do I do what's right for the workers but honor my dad as well?"

Michelle smiled knowingly, her warm brown eyes crinkling at the corners. "Delilah, I have absolute faith in you. It's a difficult situation for sure, but I know that whatever decision you make will be rooted in what's best for Alexandria Meat and all those it holds dear. You can do this."

In the dimly lit corner of O'Malley's, Delilah barely noticed Michelle's sketchbook resting on the edge of their table. Michelle picked it up, noticing Delilah's gaze on it, and she pulled a pencil from her purse and opened up the sketchbook.

"I just have to put the finishing touches on this one," she said, her pencil moving over the page.

The scent of coffee and the sound of Irish music lent a comforting air to the room. Michelle's fingers danced nimbly across the page, creating delicate strokes that gradually formed a breathtaking city skyline. The intricate detail in each building was astounding—a testament to her artistic genius.

When she was finished, Michelle handed the book to Delilah to look through.

"Michelle, these are amazing!" Delilah exclaimed, turning the pages to reveal stunning sketches of nature scenes. She traced her finger along the outline of a majestic tree bathed in sunlight, marveling at how lifelike the leaves appeared. "I never knew you were this talented."

"Thanks," Michelle replied modestly, her cheeks flushing with pride. "I've been working on them for a while now. It helps me clear my mind when I'm feeling overwhelmed. Or when I want to have a random adventure."

"Like the time we got lost in Paris, remember?" Delilah laughed, her eyes sparkling with mischief. "We ended up having the best day of our lives, wandering through the city and discovering hidden gems."

"Ah, yes." Michelle chuckled, nodding her head. "Only we could manage to get so hopelessly lost. But that's what made it so memorable." Their shared laughter filled the space between them, cementing the unbreakable bond they had forged over the years.

As they reminisced about their past adventures, Delilah was grateful for having a supportive friend by her side. Every inside joke and shared memory reminded her that she wasn't alone in her struggles and that she had someone who truly understood her.

"Remember the time we snuck into that exclusive art gallery opening?" Delilah grinned, recalling the exhilaration of their covert mission. "You managed to create an exact replica of the invite within minutes, and no one was any the wiser!"

"Ah, that was a good one," Michelle agreed, her eyes gleaming with amusement. "The lengths we go to for a little excitement."

"I know, right?" Delilah laughed, and Michelle nodded in agreement.

"Like our adventures in the past, we'll face whatever comes our way. It might be scary, but we'll grow stronger from it."

"Thank you, Michelle," Delilah whispered, swelling with gratitude. "I don't know what I'd do without you."

"Don't mention it," Michelle replied, squeezing Delilah's hand.

Delilah nodded, her resolve fortified by her friend's unwavering support.

"Do you want to talk about Jobe's dad..." said Michelle, her voice trailing off.

Delilah exhaled loudly, aching for Jobe's loss. She told Michelle everything she knew—how he was struggling to come to terms with the fact that his father wasn't coming back. How his funeral had been an emotional roller-coaster of grief and loss. How hard it must have been for him to say goodbye. Yet, despite all the sadness, Delilah noticed the number of people who had shown up in support of Jobe and his family. It was a beautiful reminder of how loved he was, even in times of hardship and sorrow.

"But there was something else," Delilah continued, her brow furrowing as she remembered the conversation she had overheard at the funeral. "Two were men talking at Jobe's dad's funeral about a strange person lurking around the construction site on the day of his death. I approached them later, and one of them said someone had tampered with the scaffold that Jobe's dad fell from. I went to the construction site yesterday to check it out and—there was a bunch of oil on the scaffold. It was so slippery."

Michelle gasped, her eyes widening with surprise. "That's strange. I went there too—when I first got back into town. This was before the accident happened. You know I love to draw architecture. Well, I saw the construction site while I was driving by, and I pulled over to sketch out some ideas for my art project," she explained, her voice filled with intrigue. "And I saw someone suspicious lurking around. He was wearing all black and seemed very out of place."

Delilah's heart nearly jumped from her chest. "Do you know who it could have been?"

"Maybe," Michelle replied cryptically, her eyes flicking toward the window momentarily before returning to Delilah's gaze. She leaned in close until she was basically whispering into Delilah's ear. "The man I saw at the construction site—and assuming it's the same one you overheard those men talking about at Jobe's dad's funeral—looked like Luke Belial."

"Luke?" Delilah asked, incredulous. "He works at Alexandria Meat. But that doesn't make any sense. Why would he—"

"I don't know." Michelle shrugged. "I'm just telling you what I saw. What I think I saw, anyway. It really looked like him."

Delilah thought hard. "Let's not bother Jobe with this yet," she told her friend. "If it turns out to be a coincidence, I wouldn't want to cause him any extra stress."

Michelle nodded in agreement.

"But definitely tell the police," Delilah said. "Just in case it's important information they need."

As they sat in the pub, the sound of Irish music and the din of the bar washing over them, a surge of energy shot through Delilah: an intense curiosity at first—and then a grim foreboding that made it feel like the world was closing in around her.

CHAPTER 6

The sunset cast an orange glow through the window, bathing Delilah in its warm light as she unbraided her pigtails and pulled her hair into a high ponytail. She stared at her reflection, preparing herself for the tough road ahead. It was time to take charge and save the Alexandria Meat plant, her father's legacy, from devastation.

"All right, everyone, gather 'round!" Delilah called, her voice ringing clear and strong through the noisy factory floor. The workers paused their tasks and turned to face her, curiosity clear on their faces. This was her moment to prove herself and gain their trust.

"Look, I know times have been tough," Delilah acknowledged, her eyes sweeping across the sea of faces. "But I'm here to make things right. I will fight for improved working conditions and fair wages for all of you. But I need your help too."

She sensed their skepticism but continued, fueled by her determination to honor her father. "Does anyone have ideas on how we can increase production? You scratch my back, and I'll scratch yours?"

A grizzled, experienced worker named Rosa stepped forward, her eyes meeting Delilah's with intensity. Although Rosa worked in the purchasing department, she also often helped out on the factory floor. "I've got a suggestion," she said, her voice rough and confident. "We've been using the same outdated equipment since I started here twenty years ago. If we invest in newer, more efficient machinery, we could significantly increase our output."

Delilah nodded, impressed. "Great idea, Rosa. I'll look into getting the funding we need for those upgrades. Anything else?"

As more workers chimed in with suggestions, Delilah noticed a growing sense of camaraderie and unity. Together, they could overcome this obstacle. But as the conversation continued, she couldn't shake the feeling that something darker loomed ahead.

"Remember," Delilah said, her voice tinged with urgency, "we're in this together. Let's save this plant and our town's economy. For ourselves and for our families."

The workers erupted into applause, their spirits lifted by Delilah's words. As the meeting dispersed and they returned to their tasks, Delilah felt a mixture of pride and trepidation. It was exhilarating—and a little bit scary.

"Are you sure you can pull this off?" asked Jerry, a seasoned employee who had been an ally to Delilah since the work disputes began. The concern on his face was undeniable.

"Of course," she replied. Though doubt gnawed at the back of her mind, she was careful not to let her face show it. Especially with your help." She gave him a wink.

As they walked the factory floor, Delilah reflected on her decision. Saving the plant would be an uphill battle, one with high stakes—jobs, livelihoods, and the fate of the entire town hanging in the balance. *Alexandria Meat is the largest employer in Alexandria,* she thought gravely.

But she was determined to rise to the challenge, driven by love for her father and a desire to preserve his legacy. All the while, unanswered questions swirled in her head like a storm: Who could she trust? What obstacles lay ahead? And most importantly, would she be able to navigate the treacherous waters of ambition, temptation, and adversity that awaited her?

The Alexandria Meat plant buzzed with activity, a stridency of machinery and shouted instructions filling the air. Delilah weaved through the factory floor, her high ponytail bouncing as she moved with purpose. She sensed some workers' skepticism like a heavy fog, their eyes following her every step, their whispers barely audible over the din.

"Does she really think she can save this place?" one worker muttered to another, casting a sidelong glance at Delilah.

"Better her than that snake Luke," came the reply.

Delilah's pulse quickened, her grip tightening around the stack of papers in her hand—financial reports, production schedules, and safety guidelines, all demanding her immediate attention. She shook her head, refusing to let doubt cloud her resolve.

I can do this, she thought. For Dad.

"ALL RIGHT, EVERYONE," Delilah announced, her voice echoing across the factory floor. "We need to find ways to cut costs without sacrificing quality or safety. Let's split into teams and brainstorm."

As the workers formed groups, Delilah noticed their weariness. Their faces were masked in exhaustion, their shoulders weighed down by the burden of uncertainty. It pained her to see them like this, but it only strengthened her determination to honor her father's legacy and save their livelihoods.

"Hey, Delilah!" Jerry called out from across the room, beckoning her over. "You might want to take a look at this."

They examined a spreadsheet outlining the plant's expenditures—numbers that painted a grim picture of the financial struggles they faced. Delilah's stomach churned, her brow furrowing as she scanned the rows of data.

"Where can we trim the fat without hurting the workers?" she asked, desperation seeping into her voice.

"Maybe we can renegotiate contracts with our suppliers," Jerry suggested.

"Great idea," Delilah replied, grateful for his support. "Let's get on that right away."

Keep pushing, Delilah thought, gritting her teeth as she drafted a proposal to present to their suppliers. *I won't let this place go down without a fight.*

JOBE AWOKE FROM an uneasy sleep. He was swirled with grief, as he remembered he would never see his father again. Tears stung his eyes, but he held them back—he wouldn't let go just yet. It wasn't time to break down; he needed to be strong.

No, he thought. *Allow yourself to grieve.*

He got out of bed and padded softly toward the kitchen. His loyal companion Smokey was already there waiting for him, eyes wide and tail wagging eagerly as he trotted up to greet his master. Jobe smiled despite himself—it was clear that Smokey knew what he needed most right now: some unconditional love and companionship.

So Jobe knelt down and hugged his beloved pup tightly, feeling the warmth of his fur against his cheek as he licked away all traces of sorrow from his face.

When Jobe finally lifted his head, there was a knock on the door. He looked up to see Jonathan standing on his porch, and Jobe opened the door and invited him in.

He smiled at the fact that he had just been thinking about spending time with Jonathan yesterday when he saw Delilah and Michelle at O'Malley's.

As Jonathan stepped into the living room, Jobe noticed the look of care and empathy in his eyes—a depth of understanding and compassion that could only come from a sincere friend. His gaze seemed to say: *I'm here for you, no matter what.*

Jobe was comforted by this silent exchange, but he still had so many questions swirling in his mind: How could he possibly honor his father's life? What might the future hold? Was there any hope left at all?

Without saying a word, Jobe got up to make coffee for them both as Jonathan settled onto the sofa. The two men sat in silence for a long while before finally beginning to talk about the good times they'd shared with Jobe's father...how he'd always been there when either of them needed someone to lean on.

They sat there and talked for several hours, and by the time Jonathan finally left, Jobe felt markedly recharged.

Later that day, as the sun was setting, Jobe strolled along the meandering banks of the Gozan River. He watched as the ripples of its water glistened in the waning light, his mind wandering to days gone by.

His thoughts were heavy with memories of his father—their afternoons spent fishing at this very spot, their laughter echoing across the shoreline. But that had all changed one fateful day—a tragedy that left Jobe struggling to maintain a sense of normalcy in his life.

He felt the coolness of the water on his fingertips as he dipped them in, and he gazed across the horizon. In that moment, he was overwhelmed with an intense sense of peace that only came from aligning himself with nature.

Tomorrow, Jobe decided, he would come back to this spot and honor his father's memory by fishing in his favorite spot. He smiled quietly to himself before getting up and heading home, never once looking back.

THE FOLLOWING DAY, Jobe awoke at dawn and packed up a tackle box and two fishing poles. With his puppy Smokey on a leash, they ventured back to the riverbank, ready for a full day of fishing.

Jobe sat down at the edge of the river and prepared for a long day ahead. As Smokey napped in the grass nearby, Jobe cast out his line into the water and watched as it flew gracefully through the air before disappearing beneath its surface.

He waited patiently, knowing that it might be hours before he felt anything on the other end. He spent the time admiring the beauty of his surroundings, watching as a family of ducks paddled past and birds flew overhead.

But despite the calming environment, Jobe's thoughts still lingered on his father. He wondered if he was making him proud, wondered if his dad would be pleased to see him out here fishing like this.

Time stopped as Jobe sat there with his line in the water, waiting for a bite. He started to lose hope as he considered that he'd never see his father again. But then, as tears streamed down and he began to give up, a flicker of hope came through. A bite!

THE SCORCHING SUN beat down on the town, casting a haze over the Alexandria Meat plant. Delilah wiped the sweat from her brow as she surveyed the scene—workers rushing about, the distant hum of machinery, and, unfortunately, the stench of fear in the air.

"Delilah!" called one of the workers, a burly man with grease-stained overalls. "You know they're talking about closing the plant, right? That means we're all out of jobs."

"He's right," chimed another, a woman named Mary who had worked there for over thirty years. "My husband lost his job at the mill last year. If this place closes, what are we going to do?"

"Listen, everyone," Delilah raised her voice, projecting confidence. "I know things look bleak right now, but I promise you, I'm doing everything I can to save this plant and your jobs. We're going to get through this."

"I can't believe we've gotten to this point," muttered an older worker, shaking his head.

"Please, trust me," Delilah implored. "I won't let you down."

"All right, Delilah," Jerry said, his expression a mix of hope and skepticism. "We'll give you a shot. But if you can't keep this place open, we're all screwed."

The pressure was immense. She had always been a hard worker, but this was different. These people were counting on her to save their jobs, and she wouldn't let them down. If this plant closed, the entire town would suffer—not only these workers but their families too.

"Thank you, Jerry," Delilah replied, swallowing hard. She knew she was fighting not only for herself but for her father and for the livelihoods of everyone in the room.

It was a noble cause, she knew, but if she couldn't pull through, would they all blame her?

"Okay, everyone," she announced, addressing the workers once more. "We need to come up with a plan. Time isn't on our side, but if we pool our resources and ideas, I believe we can save this plant and our town's economy."

"What do you guys think?" asked Jerry. "Any ideas are welcome—no matter how unconventional they may seem."

As the group began to discuss potential strategies, Delilah noticed the first flicker of hope ignite in her chest. She knew the stakes were high and time was running out, but with the support of these people who had given their lives to the plant, perhaps they stood a chance.

A week later, as the morning sun rose over the horizon, its rays shining over the bustling Alexandria Meat plant, Delilah went to work with good news. She stood in the center of the factory floor, clipboard in hand, as workers scurried around her with renewed purpose and determination.

"Great job, everyone!" she called out over the clamor, her voice echoing off the cold steel walls. "We've increased production by fifteen percent this week alone! Keep it up!"

"Delilah." Jerry approached her with a grin, his eyes reflecting the optimism that infused the workspace. "You should see the break room—they've put up a 'Days Since Last Accident' sign, and they're all keeping track. Morale's never been higher."

"I'm glad we could make a difference," Delilah replied, swelling with pride as she surveyed the scene before her. The once-downtrodden workers moved with newfound energy, their faces alight with hope for the future.

As the factory continued to hum with activity late into the day, Delilah found herself reflecting on the progress they'd made and the challenges that still lay ahead.

The factory floor was filled with the sound of machinery and voices as Delilah walked briskly past the assembly line, her high ponytail bobbing with each determined step. Expectation hung heavy in the air from the workers and herself. It was palpable, driving her forward.

CHAPTER 6

"Delilah!" Rosa called out, rushing toward her, a crumpled letter clutched tightly in her hand. "This just came for you."

"Thanks," Delilah replied, taking the letter and scanning its contents. Her eyes widened as she read.

The letter was a warning, urging her to back away from leading the efforts to save the plant. Someone out there didn't want her to succeed and was willing to put pressure on her to ensure that she failed.

"What does it say?" Rosa asked, clearly alarmed by Delilah's expression.

"It's nothing," Delilah lied, tucking the letter into her pocket. She forced a smile and told Rosa not to worry before turning on her heel and heading off in search of answers.

Delilah knew she had no choice but to carry on with her mission—but now she'd have to be even more careful. Someone had raised stakes.

Once away from Rosa or any of the other workers, Delilah pulled out the ominous letter and read it again.

> *It is in your best interest to step down from leading the efforts to save the plant. You are trampling on some very important toes. If you care about the plant and the workers, you will no longer get involved. Sincerely, Someone You Don't Want To Mess With*

CHAPTER 7

Luke Belial stood in the shadows, the flickering orange glow of his Zippo lighter casting eerie patterns on the crumbling brick walls. He ran a hand slowly across the flame, never flinching as the heat licked at his skin. A sinister smile spread across his face, mirroring the devilish glint in his eyes.

"What a delicate thing, fire," he mused aloud, closing the lighter with a sharp snap. "It can provide warmth and light, or it can destroy everything in its path."

His thoughts wandered to Alexandria Meat, the company that had been teetering on the edge of collapse for months now. The seemingly endless disputes between employees and upper management had only worsened the situation, which suited Luke just fine. He wanted nothing more than to see the plant crumble into oblivion.

But then Delilah Boaz had interfered, her infectious charisma and penchant for problem-solving breathing new life into the dying business. Suddenly, tensions were easing, productivity was increasing, and hope was beginning to infect the workforce like a virus. It frustrated him to no end—she was ruining his carefully laid plans.

"Delilah, Delilah…" he muttered, pacing back and forth. "How am I going to snuff out your little flame?"

He knew he needed to act quickly before her influence grew too strong. His mind raced through various scenarios, each more devious than the last. Time was running out, and the pressure was mounting.

As Luke leaned against the wall, deep in thought, a sudden idea struck him. A wicked grin spread across his face as the plan took shape, promising chaos and devastation. It was perfect.

"Sorry, darling," he whispered into the night, imagining Delilah's horrified expression when she realized what he had done. "But this town isn't big enough for both our fires."

With that, he disappeared into the darkness, his lighter clicking shut as he went off into the night.

The next morning, the clang of machinery and the scent of raw meat filled the air as Luke Belial weaved through the bustling factory floor, his eyes locked on Delilah. His pulse quickened, adrenaline coursing through his veins as he prepared to set his plan in motion. The Alexandria Meat plant was a ticking time bomb and he, the architect of its downfall.

"Rosa!" he called out, sidling up to the woman who had been working at the plant for years. "You got a minute?"

"Sure thing, Luke. What's up?" Rosa asked, wiping her hands on her apron.

CHAPTER 7

"Have you noticed how much attention Delilah has been paying to this place lately?" Luke questioned, his voice dripping with feigned sincerity.

"Yeah," Rosa replied, brow furrowed. "I've seen her around more. She's trying to help, I think."

"Help?" Luke scoffed, barely containing his disgust. He took a slow, deliberate breath, steadying himself. "Think about it, Rosa. Her own father wants the company to make more money. Do you really think she wants something different?"

"Wha—what do you mean?" Rosa stammered, taken aback by Luke's words.

"Come on," Luke pressed, drawing closer to Rosa and lowering his voice conspiratorially. "Do you honestly believe that Delilah is here for your best interests? Or is she another pawn in Abe's greedy game?"

As Rosa hesitated, doubt flickering in her eyes, Luke felt a surge of triumph. He lived for moments like this. He could see the seeds of mistrust taking root within her, and he knew it wouldn't be long before they spread like wildfire throughout the workforce. All he needed was a little more time, and the plant would be his.

"Look around," Luke urged, gesturing to the other employees who continued to labor under Delilah's watchful gaze. "Do you want them to suffer because of misplaced trust? Don't let her fool you, Rosa. This is about money and power, not your well-being."

Rosa stared at him, her expression a mix of confusion and fear. "I—I don't know what to think, Luke. She's always been nice to us—"

"Niceness can be a mask, my dear," Luke whispered, his eyes flicking to Delilah once more as she spoke with another worker. "And beneath it, some people are hiding the darkest of intentions."

As Rosa's face crumpled with uncertainty, Luke knew he had struck a nerve. He clapped her on the shoulder, offering a thin-lipped smile, and said, "Just keep your eyes open, all right? You never know who you can trust these days."

With that, he slipped away, leaving Rosa to ponder his words as they festered in her mind like a splinter buried deep beneath the skin.

As Luke retreated into the shadows of the factory, he felt a glorious and twisted sense of pride. His plan was taking shape, and soon enough, the Alexandria Meat plant would be nothing more than a smoldering ruin. From its ashes, he would build an empire unlike any Alexandria had ever seen.

Luke moved through the plant like a shadow, his whispered lies weaving themselves into the fabric of the workers' minds. He approached a group huddled around a conveyor belt, their laughter and camaraderie a stark contrast to what he intended to sow.

"Did you hear?" he asked, feigning concern as they turned to face him. "I overheard Delilah talking to her father. They're planning to cut wages and benefits even more."

"Are you sure?" one employee asked, his eyes widening with fear.

"Absolutely," Luke replied, his voice dripping with conviction. "Trust me. Like father, like daughter. They only care about their bottom line."

He left the group in stunned silence, their previous mirth replaced by an undercurrent of unease. Luke smiled as he spotted Delilah across the room, engaged in conversation with another worker. The tension in the air was palpable, and he reveled in it.

As he turned to sow more doubt among the employees, Delilah's gaze locked onto his. Her eyes narrowed as she stared at him.

Delilah strode toward Luke, her steps echoing through the plant.

"Luke," Delilah said, her voice cold and steady as steel. "I know what you're trying to do!"

"Delilah, my dear," he replied, feigning innocence. "I'm only here to check on our fine workers and see how things are going."

"Cut the act," she snapped. "I know what you've been saying about me. It stops now."

"Or what?" Luke challenged. "You'll tattle to your daddy? I'm simply telling the truth, and if you can't handle that, well...—"

"Enough!" Delilah shouted, her voice ringing through the room. The plant fell silent as all eyes turned to the pair.

"You have no idea what I'm trying to do here. You want to see this place fail—and I wish I knew why."

"What wild accusations," Luke replied smoothly. "I'm hurt, Delilah. But if it's a fight you want, then by all means, let's dance."

Her eyes flashed with determination as she glared at him. "You won't win, Luke. I'll make sure of it."

"Bold words," he taunted, a smirk creeping across his face. "But we'll see, won't we?"

AS LUKE WALKED away, Delilah's hands shook with anger. She couldn't believe his audacity, spreading lies and deceit among her father's employees. But she was determined to put an end to his machinations, whatever it took.

In the quiet of her office, Delilah reflected on the confrontation. She had exposed Luke's true intentions, but the damage he had done would not be easily undone. Trust would need to be rebuilt, and she would need allies in this battle against his twisted schemes. As she stared out the window at the setting sun, she knew that she had to rise above her adversary, no matter how difficult the road ahead might be.

And as the sinking sun painted the sky in brilliant hues, unanswered questions swirled in her mind like storm clouds, heralding the challenges yet to come.

CHAPTER 7

The following day, Delilah arrived at the plant as the first golden rays of sunlight broke through the clouds. She couldn't afford to waste any time if she was to counteract Luke's poisonous influence.

"Rosa!" she called, spotting the older woman overseeing the workers on the production line. Rosa looked up, her brow furrowed in concern as Delilah approached.

"Delilah, what can I do for you?" she asked warily.

"Rosa," Delilah began, taking a deep breath, "I need your help. Luke has been spreading lies about me, trying to turn everyone against me so he can take over this plant and destroy it."

Rosa's eyes widened in surprise. "What does he get out of destroying the plant? And why are you telling me all this?"

"Because I trust you, and I need allies who are loyal to my father and the company. I really don't know his motive, not yet, but we have to stop him before he ruins everything we've worked so hard for," Delilah explained, her voice firm and resolute.

"All right," Rosa agreed after a moment's hesitation. "I'll stand with you."

"Thank you," Delilah said, relief flooding through her. With Rosa by her side, she was more confident in her ability to rally the employees to her cause.

Now all she needed was for Jerry, the seasoned and reliable veteran of the plant, to have her back as well.

"Of course," Jerry told her when she approached him. "You know I'll stand with you."

Delilah showed him a warm smile and thanked him.

Delilah also thought it would be wise to have allies outside the plant—people she could confide in and get advice from when she needed it. Her friend Michelle would undoubtedly be one of them. The other would be Jobe.

Jobe had been one of her first confidants, after all. Early in grade school, when they had become friends, he had been the first person she had ever shared her struggles or secrets with. Years later, when their friendship brushed toward romance, he was just as supportive and encouraging. He always seemed to be there for her, and she wondered, in a moment of wistfulness, if he always would be.

But as she made her way to Jobe's house, Delilah felt a heavy weight in her chest. Jobe had recently lost his father, and it seemed so wrong to unload her own troubles onto him now when he was still grieving. But as she stood on his doorstep, ready to knock, something else weighed more heavily on her—the fact that if she didn't have an ally like Jobe by her side, somebody who believed in and supported her unconditionally, then how could she even begin to face all the challenges ahead? She braced herself and knocked.

Delilah met with Jobe and told him what was going on. Despite his own recent loss, he reacted just as Delilah knew he would.

"I'm here for you," he told her with a smile. "Let me know if you need anything."

Later that day, Delilah met with Michelle at a bustling coffee shop in town. As they sipped their drinks, Delilah filled her friend in on the situation.

"Delilah, I'm with you," Michelle promised, her eyes twinkling with determination. "Whatever you need, I'm here for you."

"Thank you, Michelle," Delilah replied, touched by her friend's loyalty.

Over the following weeks, Delilah and her allies worked tirelessly to develop strategies and gather resources to counteract Luke's plans. They organized meetings, both within and outside the plant, rallying people to join their cause. They faced challenges and obstacles, but they pushed through each time, growing more potent as a united force.

One evening, after another long day of strategizing, Delilah sat alone in her office, reflecting on her journey so far. She had formed alliances with Rosa and other employees at work, and they were fighting to save the plant from Luke's sinister schemes. But their battle was far from over, and there were still many unanswered questions about the enemy they faced.

"Is it enough?" she wondered aloud, staring out the window as the last vestiges of daylight faded into twilight. "Can we really save the plant and expose Luke's true nature?"

As the darkness crept in, Delilah wondered if their efforts would be enough to overcome the challenges ahead. Hearing commotion, she went out to the factory floor, and what she discovered nearly crushed her. She found Rosa and stood beside her as they surveyed the scene before them. The workers were in an uproar, voices raised in anger and fear.

"Whatever Luke said to them, it's working," Delilah whispered. She tightened her grip on Rosa's arm, drawing comfort from the older woman's presence.

"Look," said Rosa, pointing toward a group of workers who had begun to shove each other. The tension was rising, the air thick with the threat of violence.

"Enough!" Delilah screamed, her powerful voice cutting through the chaos. The workers paused, turning their attention to her. "We won't solve anything by fighting amongst ourselves! We need to stand together against our true enemy: Luke Belial."

A murmur of agreement rippled through the crowd, but it was clear that some still harbored doubts. Delilah knew she needed to win them over; the stakes were too high for failure.

"Rosa, I need you to help me calm things down here," she said urgently. "I'll try to address their concerns, but we can't afford more division."

"Of course," Rosa replied, her warm brown eyes offering solace in the midst of turmoil. "You can count on me, Delilah."

CHAPTER 7

As the days passed, Delilah found herself relying more and more on Rosa's support at the factory. Outside of the plant, it was Michelle and Jobe who kept her focused and encouraged.

"Sometimes I wonder if I'm strong enough for all of this," she confessed one evening to Jobe while winding down at O'Malley's Pub. "What if we can't save Alexandria Meat? What if Luke destroys everything my father built?"

"Delilah, you're one of the strongest people I know," Jobe said gently, his hand on her shoulder. "And even if you fail to save the plant, you will have fought with everything you had. That's all anyone can ask."

"Thank you, Jobe." Tears glistened in Delilah's eyes, and she hoped Jobe didn't see them. "I don't know what I would do without you."

As their bond deepened, so too did the challenges they faced. Luke's influence continued to grow, his lies poisoning more minds each day. The group struggled to counteract his manipulations while also tackling the logistical hurdles of keeping the plant operational.

One afternoon, as Delilah met with Jerry to discuss profitability, Rosa burst through the door, her face pale.

"Delilah, something terrible has happened," she gasped, her chest heaving from running. "One of our main suppliers has pulled out, saying they won't work with us anymore!"

"Luke must be behind this!" Delilah exclaimed, her hands clenching into fists. "He's trying to choke off our resources!"

"Whatever it takes, we need to find a new supplier," Jerry said firmly. "I'll get on it." And Jerry left Delilah's office with haste.

As the team dispersed, Delilah stared out the window at the gathering storm clouds, her chest heavy with responsibility. Their struggles had only begun, and there was no guarantee they would emerge victorious.

Is it enough? she pondered grimly, the pressure and tension bearing down on her. *Can we really save the plant and expose Luke?*

Delilah's heart fluttered as a caged bird as she and Rosa huddled in a dimly lit storage room of the plant. Her hands shook imperceptibly as she clutched the stack of documents they had managed to collect, one of which was a formal letter from their leading supplier declining to do business with Alexandria Meat. "All right," said Delilah, her voice low and steady. "I'm pretty sure Luke's been meddling with our suppliers. But we need to find out who's been feeding him information."

"Someone we trusted," Rosa said bitterly, her dark eyes narrowed with anger. "I saw him talking to Luke outside the plant last night."

"Who?" Delilah had to know, her mind reeling with possibilities.

Rosa's gaze dropped to the floor, and she fidgeted with her hands before lifting her eyes to meet Delilah's. "Jerry."

CHAPTER 8

The last echoes of machinery hummed and faded as Luke Belial stepped into the cavernous factory. Shadows loomed, cast by the scant moonlight that filtered through the grimy windows. He walked briskly through the sea of dormant equipment, his footsteps echoing in the stillness, feeling the emptiness like a void gnawing at his insides.

"Luke," Jerry whispered, emerging from behind a stack of crates. His voice was a tremor against the silence. "I've got the details you wanted."

"Spill it," Luke demanded, his eyes scanning the dark corners for any sign of movement. The quiet was unnerving, but they had to keep their meeting secret.

"Delilah's rallying everyone," Jerry revealed, shifting uneasily on his feet. "She's got a plan to save the plant. They're trying to find ways to cut costs and increase labor. Rosa suggested new equipment to make us more efficient since we've been using the same old machines for so long. But Delilah's looking for even more solutions."

"Is she now?" Luke mused, his mind spinning with the possibilities this information presented.

"Anything else?" he asked, not bothering to hide his eagerness.

Jerry hesitated before responding. "Abe...he's considering layoffs. But Delilah doesn't want anyone to lose their jobs."

"Interesting." Luke's thoughts whirled. A rift between father and daughter? A potential weakness to exploit? The thrill of the game sent adrenaline coursing through him. He was about to press Jerry for more when the sound of footsteps echoed through the empty factory.

The quiet footsteps landed lightly on the concrete floor, like someone was sneaking around in the shadows. The sound filled the air with anticipation, and Luke held his breath and listened intently. He heard a creaking noise from behind a distant pillar, followed by a click of metal against metal—someone was definitely there!

"Someone's here," Jerry hissed, his eyes wide with panic.

"Careful," Luke muttered under his breath. He couldn't risk being discovered. Not now, when everything was falling into place. "We'll continue this later. Get out of here."

They split up, melting into the shadows like phantoms in the night. The footsteps grew louder and closer. Luke's pulse pounded as he slithered through the darkness, the thrill of danger fueling him. He wondered who else was lurking in the factory and what their intentions were.

As he slipped out into the cool night air, questions swirled in his mind—who had they heard? What did they know? Was his plan compromised?

Only one thing was sure: the game had only begun, and Luke Belial was a master player.

IN HIS DIMLY lit study, Abe Boaz hunched over his desk, his brow furrowed in concentration. The lamplight cast a warm glow on the financial reports and list of potential layoffs that littered the antique oak surface. The clock on the wall ticked away, its rhythmic sound punctuating the oppressive silence.

Delilah had moved back home, but they only spoke to each other if it was about work.

Abe had been the owner and CEO of Alexandria Meat for years, and he was used to overcoming obstacles. But this time, it seemed no matter which way he turned, there were only dead ends. The economy had taken a toll on many businesses, including his own. Unless something dramatic changed soon, the company would be bankrupt in a matter of weeks.

He sighed heavily and rubbed his eyes wearily. Money was a problem that Abe took personally; it was his responsibility to keep the company afloat, but every day seemed to bring new troubles and worries. He feared that he might have to make some hard decisions soon, and it devastated him considering how much Alexandria Meat meant to him—it was his family, home, and livelihood all in one.

But as concerned as he was about the financial state of Alexandria Meat, Abe knew that drastic measures needed to be taken if they were going to survive and turn a profit again.

"Delilah!" Abe called, not taking his eyes off the papers in front of him. "Come in here; we need to talk."

The door creaked open, and Delilah entered, her expression bland. "I'm listening."

"Have a seat," he said, gesturing to the chair across from him. His voice was laced with weariness, his eyes shadowed by the tension of looming decisions. As Delilah sat, he continued, "I've been looking at the numbers. I don't see any other way…we may have to let some people go."

"Let people go?" Delilah's eyes widened in disbelief. "We can't do that! There has to be another option!"

Abe rubbed his temples. "I've considered everything—seeking outside investments, merging with another company…but none of it seems viable."

"Maybe there's something we haven't thought of yet," Delilah insisted, desperation creeping into her voice. "We owe it to our employees to explore every possibility."

"Of course," Abe agreed, but his tone lacked conviction as he stared at the dismal figures on the page in front of him. The weight of their livelihoods pressed down upon him, suffocating him with responsibility. He knew what had to be done, but the potential consequences haunted him.

What Delilah didn't know was that Alexandria Meat wasn't the only one with a money problem. Abe's personal finances were also in trouble. *Delilah's oblivious to this because I pay for the house and the bills, but I've been living off credit cards and bank loans for years, all while trying my best to hide it from her.*

The pressure of financial instability had been a stressful burden on Abe for many years, but now he worried if the company went under, he'd never get out of debt. His own survival, it seemed, was tied to Alexandria Meat's. He knew what he had to do to save the company, yet at what cost? Would the people be able to forgive him for cutting so many jobs?

He inhaled deeply and steadied himself—no matter what happened, he had to remain strong and get through this.

"Listen," Delilah said, leaning forward in her chair, determination burning in her eyes. "I'll work day and night if I have to. I'll find a way to save those jobs."

"Delilah, it's not that simple." Abe shook his head, conflicted. "I don't want to lay anyone off, but we have to face reality. If we don't act now, we risk losing everything."

"Then let's fight for it," she urged, her voice trembling with emotion. "We can find a solution."

Abe looked into his daughter's eyes, filled with hope and fire. Her unwavering belief in their ability to overcome this challenge was contagious. It made even him believe that maybe they could turn the tide. "I'm only talking about one or two people here," Abe clarified.

But that didn't seem to soothe Delilah's nerves in the slightest. "Even that's too many."

"We're running out of options, Delilah," Abe warned. He didn't think his daughter really understood the trouble they were all in. It wasn't only about Alexandria Meat—their own lives would be greatly affected as well. *The mortgage on the house, the bills, the food—I pay for all of it. Delilah doesn't understand that money doesn't grow on trees.*

"We'll figure it out," Delilah insisted. She rose from her chair, no doubt determined to set things right. As she left the room, Abe couldn't help but wonder—what if they failed? What if this was the beginning of the end for Alexandria Meat and the people who depended on it? What if it was the end for him too?

He stared at the door Delilah had disappeared through, considering every option he could think of. He felt a strong sense of loyalty to his employees, even if Delilah couldn't see that, and for a moment, he thought about looking for other options. But even as determination surged within him, unanswered questions loomed like specters in the dark corners of his mind. What would happen when the inevitable clash between necessity and loyalty came to a head? How far would he go to preserve the legacy he'd built? And in the end, what price would he—and those around him—be forced to pay?

Abe got up and started pacing around, the burden of his decisions weighing heavily on his shoulders. The tension knotted in his muscles, a physical manifestation of the chaos within his mind. Every option he considered seemed to lead to a dead end, each choice carrying with it the potential to devastate the lives of those who depended on him.

"God help me," he whispered, running a hand through his graying hair. "How am I supposed to choose between the lesser of two evils?"

The seconds passed, echoing through the silent room, a constant reminder that time was not on his side. He knew Delilah believed there was another way, one that would allow them to save the plant and protect their employees without resorting to layoffs or mergers. But despite her infectious optimism, Abe couldn't shake the nagging feeling that maybe they'd reached the point of no return.

What do I do? His eyes were fixed on the names laid out before him. Each one represented a family, a life that hung in the balance, their futures resting squarely on his shoulders. The responsibility threatened to suffocate him, and yet he couldn't escape the knowledge that the fate of Alexandria Meat lay in his hands.

His thoughts flitted from one possibility to another like a moth drawn to a flame. He reconsidered seeking outside investments? Would selling part of the company to strangers be any better than merging with another firm? Could he trust someone else to share the same dedication and commitment to the well-being of their employees?

"Ah!" he exclaimed, slamming his fist on the desk. "There's got to be another way."

But like the elusive sunset Delilah so loved, the answers he sought remained tantalizingly out of reach, and Abe was left grappling with the harsh reality that every option came with a price.

Sometimes, there is no perfect solution, he thought, accepting the painful truth. *But I must choose the path that will cause the least harm.*

As night closed in around him, Abe hoped the dawn would bring clarity—and perhaps, a glimmer of hope for the future.

The clock struck midnight, its metallic chime echoing throughout the dimly lit study.

Abe took a break, heading into the kitchen to grab a snack and then going out to check the mail. He spotted a letter addressed to him. When he went back inside and opened it, he saw that it was an offer to buy Alexandria Meat.

What? There's a potential buyer for the plant.

Abe ran a hand through his hair, his thoughts running as fast as his pulse. *I have to consider this option.* It might be the only chance to survive his financial struggles, where it seemed his bills and debts were insurmountable.

Of course, it could also lead to even more uncertainty and hardship for the workers, especially if whoever wanted to buy had no plans on keeping the plant open. He would tread slowly, carefully, and for now, he would tell no one.

Not even Delilah.

CHAPTER 9

The factory's machines whirred and clanged, filling the air with a sense of urgency. Delilah's breath hardly came as she confronted Luke Belial and Jerry, her voice barely audible over the noise of the factory floor. Rosa stood beside her, ready for the confrontation.

"I saw you guys meeting in secret the other night!" Delilah shouted. Luke's eyes widened in shock, his face losing color.

Jerry opened his mouth, but before he could respond, Delilah cut in, "You've been working for him the whole time, haven't you? Spying on us and lying to our faces!"

Workers around them began to take notice, their conversations reduced to murmurs as they glanced furtively at the unfolding scene.

Delilah's stomach dropped as she saw Luke smirk, his eyes darting around the room. He stepped in front of Jerry, blocking him from Delilah's view. "That doesn't mean anything," he said coldly. "We're coworkers; we could've been talking about anything."

Despair flooded Delilah's chest, and she was about to turn away dejectedly when she heard a soft whisper from behind Luke. It was Jerry, his voice shaking with emotion and fear.

"He offered me money," he said quietly so only Delilah, and not the other workers, could hear him. "He paid me for information about your plans."

Rage boiled within Delilah as she realized the extent of Luke's actions—what he had done and the extent he was willing to go to get ahead in life. He had bribed Jerry for information and would do anything to win this battle against her and Rosa.

Delilah fixed Luke with a hard stare, her blood simmering.

She had underestimated him—his ruthlessness was far greater and darker than she had imagined. He had manipulated the people around her, using them to feed his greed and power. There was no telling what else he was capable of.

Luke seized the opportunity to spread more lies, raising his voice so everyone could hear.

"Delilah and her father don't care about any of you! They're only looking out for themselves." He sneered, shooting her a venomous look.

Delilah's anger flared, but she swallowed the urge to lash out. Instead, she turned to the workers, her voice firm and sincere. "That's not true. We're trying to find a way to cut costs so none of you have to lose your jobs."

She saw the flicker of hope in their eyes, the tension in their shoulders easing slightly. But even with their support, it wouldn't be easy to save the plant—especially with Luke and his machinations working against them.

As the workers dispersed, Delilah thought about the challenges that lay ahead.

The next day, Delilah was deep in thought as she walked through the factory floor, trying to devise a way to save the plant. But as she rounded a corner, her attention was caught by a group of workers huddled around a machine. She heard them talking about the potential layoffs, and her stomach clenched.

Delilah decided to approach the workers, determined to do something to help. She inhaled deeply and stepped forward with determination. "What's going on?" she asked, looking around at each of them in turn.

The workers exchanged glances before one of them spoke up hesitantly. "I can't afford to be laid off," he said quietly.

Delilah nodded sympathetically before speaking again. "I understand that this is scary for all of you," she began gently but firmly, "but I'm here to tell you that we're going to find another way."

Delilah observed the skepticism in their eyes, feeling the prickling tension in the air. The evening sun cast long shadows across the room, intensifying the atmosphere.

"Look," Delilah said, her voice steady despite her anxiety. "We need to find a way to cut costs without sacrificing any jobs. We can do this if we work together." She paused, taking a deep breath, steeling herself for the challenge ahead. "But I can't do it alone. I need your help, your ideas."

"Sounds nice, but how?" one worker asked, folding his arms skeptically.

"By thinking creatively, finding innovative ways to produce our products more efficiently," Delilah replied, her determination shining through. "Every idea is worth considering."

The workers exchanged glances, murmuring among themselves. Delilah knew she had to convince them—not only for her father but for the entire community that depended on the plant.

DELILAH PACED THE factory at Alexandria Meat, trying her best to come up with ideas. Her relationship with her father was still non-existent, and her anger toward the situation bubbled beneath the surface.

Her eyes roamed the factory floor, taking in the whirring machines and the focused expressions of the workers. The urgency of the situation weighed on her shoulders like a leaden cloak, but they couldn't afford to be paralyzed by fear. They had to act, and they had to act now.

Suddenly, an idea struck her. Rosa had suggested upgrading their equipment to more modern models. They wouldn't be cheap, but they could save money in the long run. It was something worth pursuing at least.

There's no way Dad will approve spending any money right now.

But she had seen her father leave about twenty minutes ago, and he hadn't gotten back yet. If she had any chance of getting this approved, that chance was now.

Delilah marched into the factory's finance department. Her mind ran as she presented her case, but she was met with some skepticism from the finance manager.

Ben leaned back in his office chair, whistling at the high price tag of ordering brand-new machines. "It's a lot. Especially when the machines we have now work fine."

"I get it, Ben," Delilah replied, her words measured and firm. "But these aren't just any machines. They'll revolutionize our production process, paying for themselves within two months."

Ben's eyes widened a bit, looking impressed by the claim. He asked a few more pointed questions about her plan before finally relenting and saying, "Okay, as long as Abe's okay with it, we'll send the purchase orders for the new equipment off to purchasing."

"Yup," Delilah agreed, the guilt gripping her so tight she could barely get the words out. "This is what my father wants to do." *I'm the worst person in the world for this.*

Delilah knew that she was going against her father's wishes, and the shame of it all caused a wave of nausea to wash over her. But at the same time, she was sure that this was the right choice. She had to take this risk for the good of Alexandria Meat.

Every second seemed an eternity as she counted down the minutes until her father discovered what she'd done. She dreaded his reaction when he found out about it, but they were already practically ignoring each other, so how much worse could things get? If she and her father were going to remain at odds, at least some good would come of it.

Delilah left finance and went to the production line, thinking of her father, his unwavering determination, and the sacrifices he'd made for the plant and its people. Another pang of guilt surged through her, momentarily threatening to overwhelm her resolve.

I lied. And it's not like Father won't find out. What am I thinking?

Delilah returned to her office, feeling guilty that she had lied to get the new equipment approved. When her father returned, he would ask what happened in finance, and she would have to tell him the truth. She dreaded the thought of making their relationship even worse, but she was determined to make sure that his business and employees were taken care of no matter what.

Hours passed as Delilah sat at her desk, pondering what she would say to explain herself when her father came back. She went over every detail of their conversation in her head before finally concluding that all she could do was be honest with him and hope for understanding.

Just as Delilah was about to leave for the day, her father burst into her office, a look of disbelief on his face. "Tell me you're joking!" he exclaimed.

Guilt and shame washed over Delilah as she realized there was no way around telling him what had happened in finance earlier today. "Dad, I'm sorry," Delilah stammered. "I messed up, but I just wanted—"

"You went behind my back," Abe growled, an accusatory finger pointed right at her. "And you lied to get the equipment approved!"

Delilah wanted to hide. There was really no excuse for what she had done, and there wasn't anything she could tell her father to make it better. She had completely broken his trust.

"And we don't even have the money for all that!" Abe yelled. "And I would've told you that if you simply came to me first!"

"Dad, I'm so sorry," was all Delilah could say. "I just wanted to do something—anything to make things better."

"Well, this definitely didn't make things better! And I canceled those orders!" And Abe stormed away.

If Delilah was stressed before, she was utterly dejected now. Her shoulders slumped down, and her face fell in her hands as tears welled up in her eyes. She gathered her stuff to leave for the day, and she took a walk around the factory floor to check on the workers' morale before she left. But something strange was afoot.

As Delilah walked around the factory, she noticed that all the employees except Rosa were giving her the cold shoulder. No one would make eye contact with her, and when she tried to be friendly and say hello, she was met with mean looks.

She knew it wasn't about the equipment—they would've all been happy that she went out on a limb to get new machines. So what was going on?

Delilah finally made it back to Rosa, who was the only worker not looking away from her. Delilah asked her what was going on, and Rosa breathed heavily before she told her the truth.

"Luke told everyone that he tried to get the new equipment approved but that you and Abe wouldn't let him," said Rosa. "I'm so sorry. I tried to tell everyone it wasn't true, but a lot of workers saw Abe go to the finance department and overheard him telling them to cancel the purchase orders."

"What a little snake," Delilah spat. "We have to find a way to expose him. He doesn't care about any of the workers, and they need to know that."

Delilah glanced around the factory, taking in all the details. The workers were hard at work, their brows furrowed in concentration as they worked tirelessly to keep production going. But there was an even stronger tension in the air than before. People were whispering and casting sidelong glances at Delilah whenever they walked by.

The sound of machines grinding and whirring filled the air, along with the quiet hum of conversations between people, but it all seemed muted amidst the atmosphere of mistrust that pervaded the room.

Anger rose inside of Delilah. Luke had lied to all these people and made it seem like he was trying to help them when in reality, he was only looking out for himself. It infuriated her that someone could take advantage of these hardworking people and manipulate them into believing a lie.

She clenched her fists, feeling the heat of anger radiating through her body. She wanted to scream and demand justice for all the workers, but that wouldn't be productive either. Instead, she breathed in deeply and reminded herself to be calm.

She would find a way to prove Luke wrong so that everyone in the factory could see who he really was. It wasn't only about winning the fight against Luke; it was about making sure no one else got taken advantage of by him ever again.

Delilah had worked hard to make sure that everyone in the factory was taken care of, and she was so hurt that her efforts were going unappreciated.

"We need someone they trust to explain the truth to them," Delilah told Rosa. "Someone who can set the record straight and show them that Luke's been lying all this time. Only then will they begin to see me as an ally again."

Delilah hoped that if people heard the truth from a reliable source, someone they trusted, her efforts would be appreciated once more. Otherwise, she was afraid it might be too late for her to gain their trust again.

"The question is," Delilah posed, "who do the workers trust the most right now?"

Rosa shook her head hopelessly. "Luke."

CHAPTER 10

Delilah's heart pounded as she parked her car outside Michelle's art studio. Tall trees danced in the moonlight, casting long shadows across the brick walls. She glanced at Rosa, who sat in the passenger seat, her face set with determination. Both women knew that coming up with a plan was crucial if they were to save the plant and expose Luke's deception.

"Ready?" Delilah asked, her voice steady despite her pounding pulse.

"Let's do this," Rosa replied, and they exited the car and approached the studio door.

Inside, the air was heavy with the scent of oil paint, turpentine, and something more elusive, like the fragrance of a dream half-remembered. Faint strains of classical music drifted through the space, mingling with the sound of their footsteps on the polished concrete floor.

"Thank you for letting us meet here," said Delilah, showing Michelle a look of gratitude.

"You know I got you, babe," Michelle replied.

Delilah glanced at Rosa. "How's the company morale right about now?

Rosa shook her head slowly. "Honestly, not good."

"That's what I figured." Delilah sighed. "And they still believe Luke's lies?"

Rosa bit her lip. "Well, some of them do. Most of them. It's about 70/30 right now."

"Okay," Delilah said, thinking. "So the most important thing is regaining the trust of the workers. We can't do this without them. We have to give them concrete proof that Luke is lying."

Michelle was nodding at Delilah's words.

"And Luke's smart," Delilah went on, "so we'll have to be smarter."

Michelle grinned. "What do you have in mind?"

Delilah shrugged. "Well, we're gonna get a little dirty. Luke lies to the other workers, but every time I speak with him, he's pretty honest with me that he's up to no good. He has no problem telling me he's against the workers and me. He's got no shame. If I can bait him into having one of those conversations with me and some of the people can hear it for themselves, that'll be all the proof we need."

Rosa giggled. "You're going to set him up."

"It's the only way," Delilah said, laughing.

It was a risky move, but it could provide them with the evidence they needed to expose Luke.

CHAPTER 10

Outside, the night had descended with a gentle stillness. The light of the stars twinkled in the sky, while below, fireflies danced above the grass and wildflowers that grew around the studio. An owl hooted in the distant woods, and its call echoed through the darkness like a whispered secret.

The wind picked up, and the leaves rustled against each other as if whispering secrets of their own, joined by the creaking of branches swaying in time to an unseen rhythm.

Even with all these noises, though, there was something reassuring about being in Michelle's art studio at night, something blissfully calming about curling up on the sofas and discussing their plans in hushed whispers that were almost sacred. Here they were safe from prying eyes and ears; here they could plan without fear.

THE NEXT DAY at work, Delilah put her plan into action. They needed people to hear from Luke's own mouth that he was trying to sabotage the company, and it needed to be heard by people who were highly trusted on the factory floor.

Rosa was one of these people already and an ally to Delilah. But Delilah also asked two more people for help: an older worker named Fred who had worked there as long as anyone could remember and a younger employee named Matt who was charismatic and liked by everyone.

Delilah had asked Rosa, Fred, and Matt to meet her in her office after work for a meeting. Once inside, Rosa had been instructed to close Delilah's office door.

Delilah, sly as ever, saw Luke afterward and asked if he could meet her outside of her office in ten minutes. *That should give everyone enough time to get there.*

Delilah waited outside her office, and she could see Luke walking up to her.

Okay, Rosa, keep them quiet somehow. We can't let Luke know anyone's inside my office.

Her palms moistened, and her throat became dry. Her nerves grew as she contemplated the thought of Luke finding out what she was up to. She tried to steady her breathing, but it was no use—a heavy knot had formed in the pit of her stomach, and it seemed to be growing by the moment.

The sun shone brightly through the windows, throwing its light into every nook and cranny of the factory. The sound of birds chirping outside provided a pleasant backdrop for Delilah's anxiety, yet it did little to quell it.

Delilah glanced at her office door, hearing talking coming from inside. She panicked a little, but as Luke walked up, the sounds dissipated until there was nothing but silence from the other side of the door.

Delilah set the stage. "I wanted to wait until everyone left so we could really get to the bottom of things. I've been thinking about the plant and what we can do to save jobs."

Luke motioned to her closed office door. "Shall we go in?"

Delilah shook her head casually. "No need. This will be quick. What it boils down to is, I just don't think you're doing your part."

"Really?" Luke raised an eyebrow, clearly intrigued by what she had to say. "Well, it's not really my responsibility now, is it?"

As they delved into a heated conversation about the future of the plant, Delilah skillfully steered the discussion toward the workers' well-being. She could sense Luke growing more defensive by the second, and she knew it wouldn't be long before he cracked.

"You don't even care about the workers, so what do you get out of this?" she challenged, her tone a mixture of accusation and curiosity.

"Of course, I don't care about the workers!" Luke snapped, and he shook his head as if even considering it was ridiculous. "And don't worry about what I get out of this."

Delilah's heart leaped in her chest. But she didn't let her excitement show. Instead, she continued the conversation as though nothing had happened until she could safely excuse herself. Once Luke had left, she opened her office door and shook her head at the guests. "Sorry about that," she said.

Fred and Matt looked appalled. "Was that Luke who said that?" asked Fred, his old voice shaking.

Delilah nodded solemnly.

"Wow, what a great guy," said Matt.

"Tell me about it," said Delilah.

As Delilah left the building, her thoughts swirled at a breakneck pace. She had managed to expose Luke to the company's trusted workers, but would it be enough?

She knew the answers would come in time, but for now, she held onto the small victory she had achieved. It was a step forward, a ray of hope amid the darkness. She would cling to that hope as they continued their fight against the cunning and dangerous Luke Belial.

As the sun began its descent, casting long shadows across the ground, Delilah followed Rosa to her modest home on the outskirts of town.

LUKE TAILED DELILAH as she pulled away from Alexandria Meat, and he noticed that she was following Rosa, who had pulled out seconds before her. *What are you two up to exactly?*

He had a strange feeling about the conversation he'd had with Delilah in front of her office—there was something deeper at play here. He made sure he stayed far enough away and with several cars between them so as not to be noticed. Before long, Delilah and Rosa both pulled up at Rosa's home.

Luke pulled into the parking lot of a store on the corner, with a clear vantage point of Rosa's home. Rosa parked her car and got into Delilah's vehicle. As he watched them pull away from Rosa's home, a spark of curiosity ignited within Luke. He wanted to know the truth, whatever it may be. Without another thought, he started his car and followed after them into the night.

The drive felt shorter than it should have been; before long, Luke found himself on a deserted stretch of road outside Mount Moriah. Delilah and Rosa pulled over at an old art studio tucked away between towering trees and lush foliage, its windows so dark that it almost looked abandoned.

Luke parked his car in the shadows and stepped out carefully, holding his breath as he made his way toward the studio. He crept closer, taking care not to make any noise that might alert them to his presence. When both women were inside, Luke crept up to the small wooden building.

He could hear Delilah's voice coming from inside, as well as Rosa's and another woman he didn't know.

As they continued their discussion, Luke pressed his ear against the rough wooden exterior of the studio, straining to hear every word. His jaw tightened when he heard something important.

"Yeah, I got Luke to admit he didn't care about the workers," Delilah was saying. "What he didn't know was that Fred, Matt, and Rosa were right inside my office, and they heard everything."

Luke growled, his eyes glinting with the anger of a burning fire.

He couldn't let them ruin his plans—he had come too far for that. As he huddled there, his hand brushed against the studio's outer wall. It was all wood—and very, very dry.

Luke grinned, and he flicked open his Zippo lighter.

DELILAH EXCITEDLY RECOUNTED her successfully executed plan. "We've exposed him," she told Rosa and Michelle. "And now we aren't the only ones who know he's up to no good."

"But will Matt and Fred spread the word?" Michelle asked.

"Oh, definitely," said Rosa, nodding. "And so will I. People talk; it's certainly going to get around."

A sudden scent invaded their conversation. Delilah frowned, her senses heightened. "Do you smell that?"

"Smoke," said Rosa, and she looked around the room.

"Fire!" Michelle cried out as tendrils of smoke began to snake into the room. Panic crackled through them all like an electric current.

"Go! Go!" Delilah yelled, her mind racing with possible escape routes. They scrambled for the exit.

Delilah's lungs were already struggling, her chest tightening with each gasping breath. The three women burst through the door, coughing and wheezing as they sought refuge from the engulfing flames.

CHAPTER 10

"Is everyone all right?" Delilah asked, scanning her friends for signs of injury. Relief washed over her as they nodded, but then a grim uneasiness gripped her as she thought about how the fire could've started.

CHAPTER 11

Night had fallen, and Jobe sat alone on the floor of his dimly lit living room, the flickering candlelight casting ghostly shadows on the walls. He cradled a photo of his father in his hands, feeling the grief weigh down on him. His eyes were red and swollen, but he had no more tears to cry.

He felt restless, and he had recently discovered that going on a long drive cleared his mind and helped him settle down. So he got in his car, left Smokey at home, and drove away from Alexandria toward Mount Moriah. After about twenty minutes, he made a random turn onto a dark and empty street. He immediately thought that the area looked familiar. *I think Michelle has her art studio somewhere around here.*

Suddenly, his thoughts were shattered by the sight of thick smoke in the distance. Jobe pressed his foot down heavier on the pedal, speeding over the road until he saw a building on fire, the flames flashing in the night.

Adrenaline shot through Jobe as his firefighter instincts kicked in. He sped up to the structure, pulled over quickly, and got out the fire extinguisher he kept in the trunk of his car. He rushed over to the burning building and was surprised to find that it was, indeed, Michelle's art studio!

The night air washed over him as he sprinted toward the burning building, a tornado of questions swirling in his mind. How did the fire start? Was this an accident or something more sinister? And most importantly, was everyone safe?

As he turned the corner, Jobe sank at the sight that greeted him. The once vibrant art studio was now on fire, the flames licking hungrily at the wood. He could make out the silhouettes of Delilah, Michelle, and someone else huddled outside, the terror on their faces illuminated by the firelight.

"Delilah!" Jobe yelled as he approached them. She looked up as relief washed over her features. Without wasting another second, Jobe attacked the flames with the fire extinguisher, and the blaze fought back fiercely. While the fire extinguisher might not be enough to completely quell the fire, he wanted to mitigate as much damage to Michelle's studio as he could. At least until fire trucks showed up.

"Stay back!" he shouted to Delilah and the others as he continued to spray the fire. He had put out some of the flames around the bottom of the building, but the fire was still burning bright on the roof. He was relieved to hear a firetruck's siren wail in the distance and even more so when the siren grew louder and closer, signaling that they were almost there.

CHAPTER 11

"Jobe!" Delilah cried, throwing her arms around him. Her embrace was tight and desperate, exposing her fear that if she let go, he might disappear. He held her close, his eyes still scanning the scene for any signs of danger. Who or what could have caused this?

"Is everyone okay?" Jobe asked, his voice hoarse from the smoke.

"We're all right," Michelle confirmed, her face streaked with soot and tears.

As the firetruck finally arrived, its lights painting the night red and blue, Jobe felt an uneasy sense of foreboding. This fire raised more questions than answers, and he knew there was a fight ahead of them. But for now, all he could do was hold Delilah tight, grateful that they had survived this ordeal and determined to protect her no matter what came next.

"Thank you, Jobe," Delilah said excitedly, her eyes welling up with tears. She hugged him tighter than ever before, and then she pressed her lips against his in a tender kiss.

THE NEXT DAY, the factory was abuzz with whispers and rumors, each employee confiding to the next, asking if they'd heard the despicable words uttered by one of their own employees: "Of course, I don't care about the workers."

Delilah was happy to see, as she came into work, that it was all anyone was talking about. Even her father, whom she seemingly hadn't spoken to in ages, came up to ask her about it.

"Delilah, is it true that…" Abe started but couldn't finish the sentence.

She nodded. "Yes, Dad. It's true. Luke doesn't care about any of us."

"I can't believe this," Abe grumbled, clenching his fists. The workers murmured amongst themselves, their expressions a mix of anger, hurt, and betrayal.

"Is everyone just going to stand around and let this happen?" Delilah shouted over the noise, her eyes blazing. "We need to fight back!"

"That's right!" one of the workers yelled, and the others joined in, their voices rising in agreement and determination.

As the workers rallied behind her, hope swelled within Delilah. Together, they might just stand a chance against Luke and his twisted plans.

Abe's gaze met Delilah's, and she saw the protective fire burning in his eyes. He would do whatever it took to keep her safe and uphold the values he held dear—she knew that. Delilah felt a fierce gratitude towards her father, knowing that he would stand by her side no matter the cost.

"All right! Let's gather our evidence and make sure we expose Luke for who he truly is!" Abe declared, his voice filled with determination. The workers cheered in response, their spirits ignited by Delilah and Abe's unwavering resolve.

Then everyone got quiet, and Delilah looked to see Luke walking up.

"Perfect timing, sir," she said to him.

Luke looked around and took in the expressions around him. He wore a confused face, looking entirely shocked to see Delilah there. Then, as if slowly coming to understand what was happening, he began to shake his head. "Look, I don't know what she told you, but—"

"Save it, Luke. Enough people here heard you say it. Unless you're calling them liars?"

"Yeah, maybe they are," said Luke, and he started to leave the factory floor.

"Wait, Luke, you can't just walk away!" Delilah shouted as she chased after him. His face was red with fury, and his eyes burned with a fierce determination.

"Oh yes, I can," he spat back, slamming the factory door behind him. The workers inside continued to murmur amongst themselves, casting suspicious glances at the now-empty doorway.

"I believe he said it," one worker whispered to another. "Matt wouldn't lie."

"Exactly," the other replied. "And Fred's been working here forever. He'd never lie about something like that. And Rosa heard it too."

Delilah stood outside the factory. She clenched her fists, anger and frustration burning through her. This wasn't over, not by a long shot. She turned on her heel and marched back toward the factory, her resolve unwavering.

LUKE SPED AWAY in his car, leaving a trail of dust behind him. On the outskirts of Alexandria, he pulled over and slammed his fist against the steering wheel in frustration. His plan to take over the factory had been ruined by Delilah, and now he was determined to get revenge. He reached into his pocket for his lighter—playing with fire always made him feel better—but it was gone.

Luke growled. Where had he left it?

He racked his brain, trying to remember the last time he'd seen it. He must've left it at the factory.

A wave of panic washed over Luke—he always kept his lighter close by and felt naked without it. He pounded his fist against the steering wheel again, letting out a loud curse as he did so.

Still, losing his lighter was only a minor inconvenience compared to what else had happened that day. Delilah had exposed him for who he truly was and ruined all of his plans—an unforgivable sin in Luke's eyes.

He would make her pay for this, no matter what it took.

With growing rage, Luke drove to a nearby store to purchase another Zippo lighter. He quickly spotted one that had the image of a rising sun on it and grabbed it off the shelf. "This one will do nicely," he muttered to himself, his features twisted in a sinister smirk.

He paid for it and then headed back to his car, lighting the lighter and watching the fire dance as he moved his fingers through the fire.

As he looked at the flame, Luke's mind began to race with ideas. He knew that Delilah would never back down and that she was determined to make sure Alexandria Meat succeeded.

He thought of all the ways he could make her pay—from sabotaging her supplies to intimidating her workers. As he considered each of these options, his ambition grew stronger and stronger. Yes, he would bring Alexandria Meat to its knees no matter what it took!

They see jobs and the livelihood of a town, but all I see is real estate. I want that building. So much money to be made—way more than what a meat plant can bring in, that's for sure.

Another idea came to Luke.

He could make a solid case to Abe at the upcoming board meeting, telling him how unprofitable the company had been lately and that it would be better for everyone if he sold the company or laid off some of its workers. He was sure that his words would convince Abe to take action and give in to his demands.

He also knew Abe was having money problems, so selling the company was probably looking more and more attractive by the day. He could make Abe an offer, but he had to wait until Abe was desperate—until he'd already agreed to sell. *He might turn me down for the sake of his pride—especially now with this feud I've got with Delilah.*

But Luke was determined to own that building, just like he was determined to buy that plot of land where Jobe's father was trying to build a church. There wasn't much real estate for sale in the area, and he would buy up everything he could to turn a profit.

With that, Luke drove away. He settled his weight down hard on the pedal, accelerating faster and faster down the street, almost in a manic state. He put the pedal all the way down to the metal, yelling with joy out the windows. In a craze, he laughed hysterically. The wind rushed past him as he sped through red lights and whizzed around turns, leaving behind a cloud of dust as his car careened down the road.

He had been dealt a lousy hand today, but he refused to be brought down by it. If he wanted something badly enough, no force on earth could keep him from getting it. He was determined to do whatever it took to make his dreams become reality—even if it meant burning down everything in his path.

CHAPTER 11

He was coming upon a residential neighborhood, but he hardly slowed down. The houses on the street whizzed by in torpid blurs, one image after the other, flashing by again and again.

"Yeahhhhhhh!" Luke yelled, laughing all the time. "Yeaahhhhhhhh!"

Then a flicker danced in his vision, a figure walking in the middle of the street. Luke slammed on his brakes.

The car screeched to a halt, the tires squealing against the pavement. Smoke wafted up behind the smell of burnt rubber as the car came to a stop directly in front of a little girl.

"Hey!" Luke yelled at her. "What are you doing in the middle of the road? Who do you think you are?"

The girl looked at him, calmer than a person should be after that close call. She smiled at him, her slanted eyes squinting as she grinned. "I'm Mippi," she said simply. "And you should slow down, mister."

Without another word, the girl walked to a nearby house and went inside.

"I should slow down?" Luke yelled, now talking to no one. "You should get out of the street!"

Luke punched his steering wheel and peeled off down the road.

PATH BLOCKED

5

ABE SAT ALONE in his living room. He was relieved that his daughter hadn't been hurt in the fire. The revelation of Luke's true feelings had shaken him to the core. He knew he needed to support Delilah in saving the plant. More than that, though, he needed to mend what was broken between them.

Abe thought about potential strategies and scenarios, each more complex than the last. He knew that they were up against a formidable enemy, but he also knew that his daughter was strong and resourceful. They would find a way to overcome this challenge.

Abe paced back and forth in the dimly lit living room, thinking of Delilah and her recent struggles. He clenched his fists, frustration gnawing at him as he thought about what Luke had said.

"Father?" Delilah's voice cut through the silence.

Abe looked up, startled, to see his daughter standing in the doorway, her eyes filled with concern. He swelled with love and protectiveness, but he knew he couldn't let her see the turmoil raging within him.

"Delilah," he said, forcing a smile. "What's going on?"

"I wanted to make sure you're okay."

"Of course, I'm fine," he assured her, brushing off her concerns. "I'm more concerned about your well-being. That fire must've been scary."

CHAPTER 11

"It was wild, Dad," said Delilah with a slow nod.

Abe went over to Delilah and hugged her. "I'm so sorry, Delilah." He shook her gently. "I'm so sorry."

"Me too, Dad," said Delilah. "I've missed you so much."

Abe saw tears in his daughter's eyes, and it broke his heart. "Thank you for everything you've done for Alexandria Meat. You've kept the place going. Now I'm going to help. You and me," he told her, wiping a tear that rolled down her cheek. "We're going to make things right."

Delilah nodded, her eyes fixed on his. "You and me, Dad."

"This Luke is a poison to the company. We have to get him out of there."

Delilah dipped her head, her jaw set with determination. "So, what's the plan?"

"First, we make sure our witnesses are willing to speak out," Abe began, his resolve hardening. "Then, we'll bring them to human resources. It should be enough to get him terminated."

"Okay, Dad. I trust you."

"Good," he replied, pulling her into another tight embrace. "Now, let's get to work."

Just then, there was a knock on the door. Abe and Delilah jumped at the sudden interruption, their eyes wide with surprise. Who could be coming to visit them at this hour?

Abe hesitantly opened the door to find Jobe standing on their doorstep.

"Jobe, come in!" said Delilah, motioning for him to enter. She gave him a quick hug, and they all sat down.

"What is it, Jobe?" Abe asked, his voice steady despite the surprise.

Jobe looked solemnly at the pair before him and cleared his throat. "At Michelle's art studio," he said, his voice heavy with importance. "After the fire department put out the fire, they wanted to ask me a few questions since I tried to help stop the blaze. Because of my firefighting background, they asked if I had any clues on how it started. I noticed that the fire marshal found something on the ground—a Zippo lighter with an engraving of a snake on it."

CHAPTER 12

Jobe stood in his living room, staring at the framed photograph on the wall. His father was looking at him in the picture, it seemed, the stoic look he always had, his arms crossed over his chest. Jobe found himself wanting to connect with him, to honor, to grieve him. All these things made him think of how Delilah was handling the split with her own father. The sun was just beginning to rise, casting a warm glow across the room. As he thought about Delilah's unwavering commitment, he realized that he owed it to his own father—and to himself—to do the same. *She's honoring her father by trying to save the meat plant. And I can do the same.*

His mind drifted to the small church his father had been building near Mount Moriah.

He had once hated that church—the construction site—the very street it was on. It reminded him of his father being taken away from him. But now he saw it as something else. It was part of his father's legacy and a way to be close with him even now, when he no longer breathed.

"Come on, Smokey!" Jobe called to his puppy, who wagged his tail enthusiastically. "We've got work to do."

Smokey followed him out the door, barking playfully as they got in Jobe's car and drove toward Mount Moriah. On the drive there, all Jobe thought about was the unfinished church that his father had started building. It had been his father's dream to create a sanctuary where the community could come together, and Jobe knew it was time for him to step up and see that dream fulfilled.

Arriving at the construction site, Jobe got out and surveyed the half-built structure before him, determination settling in his chest. He picked up a hammer, feeling its weight in his hand.

I've learned to grieve my own way, and now I need to take action to honor my father's memory.

"All right, let's get this place finished," Jobe declared to the empty lot, his voice echoing off the surrounding hills.

He began making calls, re-hiring the workers his father had originally contracted, each one eager to return to the project. They arrived one by one, tools in hand, ready to help Jobe complete the church that would stand as a testament to his father's memory and their collective resolve.

As they worked, word spread throughout the town, and soon Jobe found himself joined by Jonathan, Delilah, Michelle, and Abe. They had heard about his efforts and came to lend their support.

CHAPTER 12

"Jobe, this is amazing," Delilah said, her eyes shining with admiration as she looked around at the bustling construction site. "Your dad would be so proud."

"Thank you," Jobe replied, the corners of his mouth lifting into a small smile. "I think he would be, too."

As evening came, a sense of peace washed over Jobe. For the first time since his father's death, he knew without a doubt that he was doing exactly what he was meant to do. He glanced up at the sky, where the first stars were emerging, and whispered, "We're going to finish it, Dad. I promise."

Jobe spent the next day working on the church as well, along with the other workers he had rehired. As he hammered a nail into a wooden beam, he couldn't ignore the churning emotions threatening to overwhelm him. His father's absence hung heavily in the air, and he found himself questioning whether this was what his father would have wanted.

"Focus, Jobe," he whispered to himself, wiping the sweat from his brow.

But those thoughts were quickly replaced by another lingering question—his feelings for Delilah. Her passion, unwavering loyalty, and fierce determination stirred something deep within him. But could he allow himself to pursue her while grappling with his grief and the responsibility of honoring his father's memory?

"Need a hand?" Jonathan called out, snapping Jobe back to reality.

"Sure," Jobe replied, grateful for the distraction.

Jonathan, Delilah, Michelle, and Abe approached, each carrying tools and wearing determined expressions.

"Jobe, we're here to help," Delilah said, her eyes softening as she looked at him. "This is important to all of us."

"Thank you," Jobe said, his voice thick with emotion. "I appreciate it."

They worked tirelessly, hauling lumber, sawing wood, and hammering nails. The sun blazed overhead, but the intensity of their labor matched the fire burning within them. Each swing of the hammer, each plank secured in place, brought them closer to fulfilling the dreams of their lost loved ones.

As the day wore on, the physical exhaustion began to dull the sharp edges of Jobe's emotional turmoil. In its place, a sense of unity and shared purpose took root. He couldn't deny the connection he had with Delilah, but he also realized that their bond was forged in the crucible of shared loss and determination to honor the legacies left behind.

"Jobe," Delilah said, resting a hand on his shoulder. "You're doing an incredible job here. Your father would be so proud."

"Thank you, Delilah," Jobe said, feeling a knot form in his throat. He knew she was right. They were bringing the community together, finding strength in each other during these dark times. For now, that was enough.

As the sun began to set, Jobe took a moment to catch his breath. His body ached and his heart was heavy, but as he looked around at the progress they had made, he felt something he hadn't experienced in a long time—hope.

I'll keep pushing forward, Dad, he thought. I'll make sure this church stands tall as a beacon of hope for our community.

THE NEXT MORNING, Delilah was sore from helping Jobe on the construction site the day before. Every muscle in her body ached, but it was a good ache. She had done something meaningful, and the knowledge that Jobe appreciated her help meant even more to her.

She stretched her tired arms above her head and let out a satisfied sigh. She couldn't help wishing that this new routine could last forever—working alongside Jobe in peace and contentment, surrounded by their friends who were becoming family.

But Delilah knew that life was unpredictable at times, and a sense of foreboding mixed with anticipation lingered in the air. Something was coming—she just didn't know what yet. But if Jobe had taught her anything, it was to never give up hope, no matter how dark things may seem. With new strength, Delilah stepped into the day, ready for whatever came next.

She drove to work, put on her apron, and clocked in at Alexandria Meat, almost forgetting about the silver Zippo lighter that Jobe had told her about. It was the one he found at Michelle's art studio the night of the fire. Whoever had dropped the lighter must have been the person who started the fire.

Delilah thought about the description Jobe had given: a silver Zippo lighter with a snake etched into it.

Delilah described the lighter to several of her co-workers, and everyone she told about it said the same thing: it was Luke's signature Zippo, one he played with often.

"Oh, that's Luke's," said a random employee Delilah had approached. "Right?" he asked uncertainly, as if he might've made a mistake by doing so.

"It sounds like Luke's," another worker told her.

"Isn't that the lighter Luke's always playing with?" said another.

And finally, Delilah's trusted ally, Rosa. "It's Luke's all right," she said with a grave look in her eye.

Delilah shivered. She had suspected Luke of a lot of foul things when it came to bringing the company down, but nearly burning them to death? She never imagined it. But here it was, all the evidence pointing to him as the culprit. A whirlwind of emotions stormed within her—shock, anger, betrayal—all washing over her at once.

Her stomach churned as she thought about how Luke could've done something like that—they could've been killed! Delilah's head spun with questions and disbelief as she tried to wrap her brain around the situation before her.

And then she remembered something else, the figure that had been spotted at the construction site the day of Jobe's father's death. Michelle had said that it looked like Luke, and Delilah had examined the construction site to find the bottom of the scaffold slick with oil. She now considered, her chest tight with dread, that Luke might have been the orchestrator of many unspeakable things.

She looked around the factory, suddenly feeling a sense of broad danger. Everything had appeared so safe and familiar before, but now it seemed a place of terror. She considered that Luke was far more dangerous than she had ever imagined, and she quickly made her way out of the factory and into the safety of her car. As she drove away, all Delilah thought about was how lucky they were to have survived the fire—and how lucky they would all be if they never encountered Luke again.

Delilah knew that she needed to tell Jobe the truth about Luke and what had happened, but she couldn't bring herself to ruin his newfound peace. He had worked so hard to cope with his grief and build something good out of the rubble of tragedy, and she didn't want to take that away from him. She only hoped that whatever was coming wouldn't be a threat to what they had built together in their little corner of the world.

Delilah drove home with a heavy heart, unsure of what would come next—but determined to make sure Jobe and everyone else remained safe regardless. When she got home, she changed her clothes and then headed off to the church to help Jobe.

AN AMBER GLOW from the setting sun bathed the half-finished church in a warm light, and Jobe felt an undeniable sense of peace wash over him. With every swing of the hammer, he felt more connected to his father's memory than ever before. This was the first time since his father's death that he had allowed himself to feel this way, and it was as if he could hear his father's voice whispering in the wind, telling him that he was on the right path.

"Jobe!" Jonathan called out, patting him on the back with a smile. "We should probably call it a day. It's getting late."

"Yeah, you're right," Jobe agreed, his hands calloused and sore from the day's labor. They packed up their tools and said their goodbyes to Delilah, Michelle, and Abe.

"Thank you all for coming out today," Jobe said sincerely. "It meant a lot to me."

"Of course, Jobe," Delilah replied, her eyes shimmering with emotion. "We're here for you, just like you've been there for us."

Jobe felt a strange sense of unease, as if Delilah was hiding something from him. He had known her since they were kids and could always tell when she was holding back.

But he didn't mention it—he only smiled at her warmly and said his final goodbyes before heading home.

As Jobe drove, his mind exploded with questions. What was Delilah hiding? What had happened in the factory? There seemed to be something going on that none of them wanted to talk about.

As Jobe walked through the twilight toward his house, he felt his father was right there with him. The air was crisp, the sky a deep indigo, dotted with the first stars of the evening. He wondered if his father was watching over him from somewhere among them.

Reaching his porch, he leaned against the railing and gazed at the heavens. The words came unbidden, spilling from his soul. "I worked on the church today, Dad," he said to the sky. "And I'm going to finish it. For you."

A sudden gust of wind rustled the leaves around him, and for a moment, he felt a gentle embrace from his father. Tears welled up in Jobe's eyes, and he allowed himself a moment of vulnerability.

"Thank you, Dad," he whispered. "For everything."

Jobe's gaze followed the trail of stars across the night sky until it fell upon a single, brilliant point of light. *Polaris,* he thought to himself, recalling his father's lessons on celestial navigation. *The North Star.* The unwavering beacon shone down upon him with the steadfast guidance his father had always provided. He smiled as he felt his father's presence with him, watching over him from above.

"All right, Dad," he whispered, clenching his fists at his sides. "I've got this."

With newfound determination, Jobe stepped inside the house and walked straight to his father's bedroom. The room was steeped in memories, each item holding a story of its own. Jobe could almost hear his father's voice echoing through the space as he glanced around.

He opened his father's dresser and began rummaging through the contents, searching for something—anything—that might bring him closer to his father in his absence. As he shuffled through old photographs and mementos, his fingertips brushed against a folded piece of paper tucked away in the corner.

"What's this?" he muttered, his curiosity piqued. Unfolding the letter, his eyes scanned the contents carefully.

It was an offer to buy the vacant lot where the church now stood. Jobe's brow furrowed. The gears in his head turned, trying to piece together the puzzle before him.

While it was apparent his father hadn't accepted the offer, Jobe was still curious as to who would want to buy that plot of land.

As he looked at the bottom of the letter, he saw that it was signed: Luke Belial.

CHAPTER 13

Abe Boaz paced the floor of his office. He knew he had to contact the supplier who had recently cut ties with Alexandria Meat. Sweat beaded on his forehead, and his hand trembled ever so slightly. Something was off about the whole situation, but he didn't have the evidence to prove it. Not yet.

So he drafted a letter to Reynold Distribution, asking why, after doing business with them for nearly ten years, they had refused to continue working with Alexandria Meat. He sent the letter and checked his mail every day for a response.

It wasn't long before he received one.

A little over a week later, a letter from Reynold Distribution appeared with the incoming mail.

Abe opened the letter and it read: "Not long ago, we received a letter that stated you would only continue to do business with us if we dropped our prices by fifty percent. This was not a request we were willing to accommodate. We found the letter to be unusual, considering our long history of business, but it did appear to be signed by you, Abe. We kept the letter, and I've included it for your review. Kind regards, Sam. Reynold Distribution."

Abe's mind reeled, his fingers trembling as he opened the folded-up letter tucked in the envelope. It was true, he saw as he read the letter. As Abe saw his forged signature at the bottom, his hand squeezed into a fist, the letter crumpling in his grip. Then he calmed himself and uncrumpled the letter, spreading it out and smoothing the wrinkles. He would need it for evidence.

Could this be...Luke?

Abe went through his files and pulled out everything Luke had signed or written on—from new hire paperwork to tax forms to simple workplace notes. He compared the writing on these documents to the letter and forged signature. The handwriting looked nearly identical.

"Delilah!" Abe called, summoning his daughter into the room. "Get human resources and the management team together. We're having an emergency meeting."

AS EVERYONE FILED into the tense boardroom, Delilah looked around. Her eyes darted between her father, the managers, and the human resources representatives. Then she looked at Luke Belial and the two security guards who stood on either side of the door. She wondered if they would be needed.

They had witnesses against Luke—Rosa, Fred, and Matt, who had all heard him admit that he didn't care about the workers. But seeing her father's confidence made her think he had even more evidence than that. She wondered what he had found out.

"Thank you for coming on short notice," Abe began, his voice hard and unyielding. "We have a serious issue to discuss—corruption within our own ranks." He paused, letting the gravity of his words sink in before continuing. "I hold in my hand evidence that Luke Belial has been sabotaging our business deals."

A murmur rippled through the room as Abe held up the letters he had received from Reynold Distribution. He gave them to the other managers to look at. They shifted uncomfortably in their seats as they passed them around, ending with the human resources manager, who looked highly bothered by the evidence. Delilah watched as her father's face grew grimmer with each passing second.

"Luke doesn't care about our company or our workers," Delilah added, her voice shaking slightly. "Rosa, Fred, and Matt, as well as myself, all heard him admit this blatantly."

The room fell silent, the tension in the room palpable as everyone absorbed the cold reality of the situation.

"This man has no place at Alexandria Meat," Abe declared. "His actions have jeopardized the livelihoods of our employees and the future of our company. We must act immediately."

As the boardroom erupted into a flurry of urgent discussions and debates, they had finally exposed Luke's corruption. But what would come next? What kind of fallout would they face?

Luke's face contorted into a mask of indignation as he shot up from his seat. "This is ridiculous!" he spat, each word dripping with venom. "I don't know who doctored those letters, but it wasn't me!"

"Sit down," Abe replied, his voice steady and commanding. But Luke remained standing, his chest heaving with anger.

"Maybe you're trying to get rid of me because I'm a threat to your precious legacy, huh?" he sneered, pointing an accusatory finger at Abe. The room held its breath, the air thick with tension.

"Enough, Luke." Another manager, a stern woman in her early forties, rose to her feet. "We've heard enough evidence against you today. Your attempts to sabotage this company and undermine our workforce have been laid bare."

"Your employment here is terminated, effective immediately," Abe added, locking eyes with Luke. "Security will escort you out of the building."

"Are you all blind?!" Luke roared, his face turning crimson with rage. He looked around the room, searching for any sign of support or sympathy, but found none. Every pair of eyes that met his were filled with contempt and disgust.

"Get him out of here," Abe muttered, not breaking eye contact with Luke.

As two security guards grabbed Luke by the arms, he thrashed wildly, spitting curses and insults at everyone in the room. Delilah shook her head as she watched him struggle, the raw fury in his eyes burning itself into her memory.

Finally, they dragged him from the room, his furious shouts echoing through the halls long after the door had slammed shut behind him. Delilah exhaled deeply, her hands shaking from the intensity of the confrontation. She glanced over at her father, whose expression was a mix of relief and exhaustion.

"Thank God that's over," she whispered, her voice trembling. "I just hope we can recover from the damage he's done."

Abe nodded solemnly, his eyes distant. "We'll find a way to move forward. That's what we do. We adapt, and we overcome." His voice was quiet but firm, reflecting the steely determination that had made him a successful businessman over the years.

As the room began to empty, Delilah couldn't help but wonder: would things ever be the same again? Had they really seen the last of Luke's treachery, or were there still more secrets waiting to be uncovered? And in the face of all this uncertainty, how could they possibly hold onto hope?

"Delilah," Abe said gently, placing a hand on her shoulder. "We'll get through this. As a family. Remember—no matter how dark things may seem, there's always a light at the end of the tunnel. We have to keep moving forward."

And with those words, Delilah found herself clinging to a fragile sense of hope—a hope that carried with it a thousand unanswered questions and a world full of unknowns. But perhaps, in the end, that was enough.

ABE SLAMMED THE front door behind him as he processed the whirlwind of emotions from the day's events. He strode into his home office and took a seat, glancing at a photograph on his desk—a candid shot of Delilah laughing in the golden glow of a sunset. He clenched his fists, fighting to stay grounded in the present moment.

"Keep moving forward," he muttered under his breath, echoing the words he had spoken to Delilah earlier.

There was a letter on his desk. Delilah must've checked the mail earlier and left it for him. It was from the interested buyer of Alexandria Meat who had reached out before. His pulse quickened as he opened the letter, his eyes scanning the text for any indication of the buyer's intentions.

Just then, Delilah walked in and saw the letter Abe was reading. "What's that?" she asked in a quiet voice.

"It's an offer to purchase the company," Abe said without looking up from the screen. He hesitated, unsure of whether or not he should trust Delilah with this sensitive information. But before he could make his decision, she spoke again.

"Will you let me do something, Dad? Will you let me negotiate a deal that will be mutually beneficial to both you and the workers?" Her eyes pleaded with him to take her seriously.

Abe looked at his daughter for a moment before finally nodding in agreement. He knew she was capable of handling this—after all, he had taught her everything she knew about negotiating deals and closing contracts. She was sharp, confident, and she had good instincts for business. He decided to trust her judgment on this matter.

Delilah smiled gratefully as Abe handed her the letter.

For the next hour, she carefully crafted a proposal. She detailed the terms and conditions of her counteroffer, emphasizing that both sides would benefit from a successful transaction. As she wrote, Abe watched nervously, afraid to breathe lest he broke her concentration. Finally, after Delilah had proofread and edited her work several times, she folded the letter and tucked it into an envelope.

PATH BLOCKED

DELILAH STOOD IN the dimly lit hallway of her home, her back pressed against the cold wall as she stared at the letter on her dresser across the room. She had mailed off the proposal to Alexandria Meat's interested buyer, but now she had a new challenge to tackle.

The flickering overhead light cast eerie shadows on the walls, reflecting the turmoil that churned within her. She felt like a hurricane trapped in a snow globe—caught between the familiarity of Alexandria Meats and an uncertain future.

Maybe you shouldn't work here anymore, her father's words echoed in her mind, stinging like a fresh wound. Delilah gritted her teeth and pushed herself off the wall, striding purposefully toward the dresser. She had taken his advice, applying for countless positions in various parts of the country and even abroad. One position in particular had caught her eye—a quality control manager role in Amsterdam. The idea of starting anew in a foreign country had ignited a spark of excitement deep within her.

"Is this really what I want?" Delilah whispered to herself, picking up the letter. She wondered what it said. A few letters had come in from potential employers, but she hesitated to open them, afraid of what they might reveal.

Nothing ventured, nothing gained, she thought, tearing open the envelope. She held her breath as she read it.

"Congratulations, Delilah," it began. "We are pleased to offer you the position of Quality Control Manager at our Amsterdam facility. Your experience and skills make you the perfect candidate for this role."

"Amsterdam," she said, the foreign city's name rolling off her tongue like a promise of adventure. Her mind filled with images of cobblestone streets and historic buildings.

As she read through the message, her eyes widened in disbelief. The offer was complete with relocation assistance and a generous salary package.

"Delilah Boaz, Quality Control Manager…" she murmured, trying the title on for size. It sounded promising, but it also meant leaving everything she had ever known—her family, her friends, and her life at Alexandria Meat.

"Sunset is a time for change," she mused, glancing out the window at the fading light. As the sun dipped below the horizon, the room was bathed in warm hues, a familiar comfort amid the chaos of her thoughts.

"Maybe this will be good for me," she whispered, her fingers trembling.

But as she stared at the letter, she couldn't shake the nagging feeling that something was amiss—a piece of the puzzle still missing.

Is this truly the right path for me? she wondered.

As darkness crept across the sky, Delilah found herself suspended between two worlds—her past and her future, each filled with their own mysteries and uncertainties. As she stood on the precipice, teetering between the familiar and the unknown, she knew that only time would reveal the answers she desperately sought.

Was she ready to leave everything behind—her friends, her family, and the only life she had ever known? The thought both exhilarated and terrified her, leaving her caught in a whirlwind of emotions.

She had to tell Michelle.

Delilah drove to Michelle's house, barely able to contain her excitement. She had never expected this opportunity would arise—a chance to leave Alexandria Meat behind and start anew in a foreign country! She wanted to tell her friend in person about the news, and nothing would stop her from doing so.

The drive was filled with anticipation as Delilah took in the sights around her, watching as the familiar scenery gradually shifted into something new and unknown. She felt a sudden influx of energy as she drove to her friend's home, finally feeling free from the confining bonds of the past few years.

The evening sky glowed with sunshine as Delilah pulled up outside Michelle's house, parking next to an old oak tree that creaked in the wind.

Taking a deep breath, Delilah stepped out of the car and walked toward the door. She savored the warmth of the evening air as she knocked on the door, filled with excitement about what this new opportunity might bring.

CHAPTER 13

Delilah knocked on her friend's door.

Michelle opened the door and smiled. "Delilah! What are you doing here?" Her voice was filled with excitement as she embraced her friend in a warm hug.

"I wanted to tell you something," Delilah replied with a smile. "I got a job offer in Amsterdam!" She laughed in joy as she shared the news, barely able to contain her excitement.

Michelle's eyes widened in surprise as she stepped back from the embrace, taking a moment to process what had just been said.

"Wow," she said in awe, a look of admiration on her face. "That's great news! We should celebrate!" She ushered Delilah into the house with an excited wave of her hand, ready for a night of adventure. "Are you going to take it?"

"I don't know," Delilah admitted, her voice barely audible as her mind bubbled with unanswered questions.

"Take your time," Michelle advised gently, placing a hand on Delilah's shoulder. "Think about what you really want, and don't be afraid to chase your dreams."

"Thanks, Michelle," Delilah murmured, grateful for her friend's unwavering support.

Change is inevitable, she thought, her father's wisdom echoing in her mind. *But is this the path I should take?* With each passing moment, the decision became even more difficult, threatening to crush her beneath its burden. *Amsterdam or Alexandria Meat?* She pondered, her mind wrestling with her choices. *What do I truly want?*

As night fell upon the world outside, Delilah Boaz found herself standing at a crossroads, unsure of which path to choose and unaware of the consequences that lay ahead.

CHAPTER 14

Voices filled the air as the workers of Alexandria Meat huddled together, their breath visible in the chilly morning air. Delilah stood before them as she prepared to deliver the announcement.

Delilah looked out over the crowd of workers, her face creased with worry. Each and every one of them was depending on her, and she wanted to do what was best for them. She cleared her throat, shifting from foot to foot as she tried to find the words that would convey what she wanted to say.

"Silence, please!" Delilah shouted above the din, her usually warm and friendly demeanor replaced by fierce determination. She waited for the murmurs to die down before she continued. "I have important news about the future of Alexandria Meat."

All around her, the murmurs faded away into a tense silence.

The crowd leaned in, clinging to every word as if it were their lifeline.

"Alexandria Meat has been sold to a new owner," she began, her words met with whispers of uncertainty.

Gasps susurrated from the crowd.

"This new owner values our community, and I have been assured by them that every single one of you will keep your jobs!"

A mix of relief and skepticism washed over the faces of the workers, their eyes searching Delilah's. It was only when they saw the sincerity in her gaze that they allowed themselves to exhale, the tension slowly dissipating.

"Are you certain, Miss Boaz?" a grizzled worker asked, his voice laced with both hope and doubt.

Delilah nodded, her eyes meeting his. "I am certain. This is not a rumor—it's a fact. The new owner believes in the potential of this plant and our community. They want to see us thrive, and they're willing to invest in our future."

The news continued to ripple through the crowd, and soon enough, the relief began to outweigh the skepticism. Workers exchanged glances, tentative smiles playing on their lips as they dared to believe that their livelihoods were secure.

"Thank you, Miss Boaz," the grizzled worker said, his voice cracking with emotion. "You've given us hope when we thought all was lost." The others murmured in agreement, the gratitude evident in their eyes.

Delilah blinked back tears, her chest tightening as her father's legacy settled upon her shoulders. She knew she had made the right decision, one that honored not only her father but the entire community that depended on Alexandria Meat for survival. As she looked out at the sea of faces before her,

Delilah realized the true power of unity and connection, understanding that it wasn't only the plant that would live on—it was her father's spirit, embedded within every worker, every family, and every corner of their small town.

"Go home to your families," Delilah told them, her voice filled with warmth and conviction. "We're giving everyone a paid day off today. Celebrate this new beginning. We've been granted a second chance, and we must make the most of it."

At her words, the crowd erupted into cheers. The tension that had pervaded moments before was replaced with joyous energy as back slaps and laughter filled the air. Tear-filled eyes smiled in abject relief, each person feeling an immense sense of gratitude for Delilah's leadership and courage. As workers celebrated and embraced each other with joyous cries of "We did it!" Delilah felt her father's legacy swell within her chest. She knew then that his legacy was safe, for she saw before her not workers but family—a family united by their shared struggle, polished by their resilience and hope.

The cheers echoed through the morning air, reverberating off the nearby buildings like a song of triumph as friends and neighbors celebrated what could only be described as a miracle. It was agreed upon by all present that this was indeed a day worth celebrating—a day that marked the beginning of something greater, something precious.

As the workers dispersed, a sense of quiet determination settled over the plant. The air seemed charged with possibility, and for the first time in months, hope shimmered like a beacon in the darkness, guiding them toward a brighter future.

Delilah dialed Michelle's number, her fingers trembling with the aftershocks of adrenaline. The phone rang once, twice, and then Michelle's voice broke through the static.

"Hey, Delilah! What's going on?" Her tone was casual, but Delilah sensed the undercurrent of concern beneath the surface.

"Michelle, we did it," Delilah said, her words tumbling out in a rush. "We saved the plant. Everyone gets to keep their jobs."

"Wow, that's amazing! Tell me how you pulled it off!" said Michelle, genuine excitement in her voice.

"Long story, but we found a buyer who shares our values and wants to keep the community intact," Delilah explained. "It feels so good to do something that honors Dad and everything he's worked for."

"Delilah, I'm so proud of you. You've shown everyone what it means to care for others and stand up for what's right," Michelle said warmly.

"Thanks, Michelle. It means a lot to hear you say that." Delilah paused, suddenly aware of how much she had relied on her friend throughout this entire ordeal. "I couldn't have done it without your support."

"Of course. That's what friends are for," Michelle replied, her voice softening. "And besides, you've always been there for me too."

As they continued to chat, Delilah realized just how much her relationships with friends and family had been strengthened during this time. She thought about her father, their relationship mended, and the newfound understanding between them.

"Michelle, thank you for everything. I've learned so much about the importance of community and connection, and I owe a lot of that to you," Delilah said sincerely.

"Like I said, that's what friends are for. We're in this together, always," Michelle assured her.

"Always," Delilah echoed, swelling with gratitude.

The next day at work was an exciting one.

"Can't believe they're actually keepin' the plant open!" one man shouted, clapping his friend on the back.

"Miracles do happen," an older woman murmured, her eyes brimming with tears as she clung to her husband's arm.

As Delilah greeted the employees, she reflected on the journey that had brought her to this moment—not only her own but Jobe's as well. Their paths had been shaped by grief, yet they had both found a way to grieve and to take action to honor their fathers.

"Delilah! Thank God you did something about this!" a voice rang out, and Delilah turned to see a young woman wearing a grateful smile. "Thanks so much!"

"Thank your new owner," Delilah said modestly. "I only spoke up for what I believed was right."

"Still, you got the ball rolling," the woman insisted, hugging Delilah tightly.

"Thank you, Delilah," another worker chimed in, offering his hand for a firm shake. "You stood up for all of us."

"Means a lot to have someone in our corner," added a third, tipping his hat in Delilah's direction.

"My dad deserves some credit too," she reminded them, her thoughts turning to her father. "He's the one who found the buyer."

"Well, thanks to both of you," the man said. "We're lucky to have people like you two fighting for us."

As the workers continued to share their gratitude, a spark of determination ignited within Delilah. There was still so much to learn about the new owner's intentions and how this change would impact the community, but as long as they stood together, they could face any challenge.

"Thank you," she whispered, her voice barely audible above the chatter and laughter of the crowd. "Thank you all for showing me that even in the darkest times, there is always hope."

Delilah was overwhelmed by the joy and gratitude that radiated from everyone at Alexandria Meats. All around her, people were celebrating, laughing, hugging and embracing each other—a stark difference from the despair she had experienced just days before.

The light of hope had returned to this small town, and for that Delilah was immensely proud. Even though she had been scared and uncertain of the future, seeing her friends and co-workers so happy made it all worth it. She smiled in contentment as she watched the people around her celebrate their recent victory. It was stunning to see that a simple act of kindness could bring so much joy to those who needed it most.

Delilah knew then that as long as they kept their faith and worked together, anything was possible.

LUKE BELIAL SCARFED down his breakfast, mind ablaze over being fired from Alexandria Meat. *What now? What's the plan?*

He could've made so much money if he had acquired the Alexandria Meat building. But that dream was gone, and it was time to move on.

Abe and Delilah Boaz. I absolutely hate them.

He finished off the remaining eggs on his plate and washed them down with a glass of orange juice. Just then, he heard a knock at the door.

Luke looked through the peephole to see a middle-aged man in a suit standing outside his door. He opened the door slowly. "Can I help you?"

The man nodded, and there was a grimness on his face that didn't sit well with Luke. He flashed a badge. "I'm Detective Parker. Do you have a few minutes?"

"Sure," said Luke. "Come on in."

The detective stepped inside and got straight to the point. "I've had two separate people come forward with suspicions that there may have been foul play in a recent construction accident regarding a deceased Mr. Johnson."

Luke couldn't believe what he was hearing. "What's that got to do with me?"

"Well, one of them said they saw you at the scene," the detective explained. "The same week of the accident. Perhaps even the night before."

Luke shrugged. "It's possible. I have a passion for real estate and often check out new buildings in the area."

Detective Parker looked at him for a few moments without blinking. "So you don't deny being there?"

"Of course not," said Luke. "I definitely checked out the construction site. So what?"

"Well, another person found oil on the scaffold, that's what."

"Oil?" Luke questioned.

CHAPTER 14

"That's right," said Detective Parker. "It tends to make things slippery. And when a guy falls off a scaffold, it starts to look a little weird if there was oil on it."

"I completely agree," said Luke. "You're not saying..."

"That you put the oil on the scaffold?" The detective chuckled. "Oh no, not at all. But it was worth asking you about." And the detective winked at him. "I'll let you know if I have any more questions."

He turned on his heel and walked out the door.

Luke didn't like this, didn't like it all. Perhaps it was time to leave Alexandria behind. He had heard of blossoming real estate opportunities in some of the big cities—New York, in particular—and thought it might be interesting to look into. He smiled. *That could be fun.*

THE WIND ROARED outside as Delilah burst through the front door of her childhood home, still buzzing from the day's events. The warm scent of freshly baked bread and sizzling onions enveloped her as she stepped into the cozy kitchen. Abe stood at the stove, his brow furrowed in concentration as he stirred a simmering pot.

"Hey, Dad!" Delilah called out, her voice shaky with emotion. Her father looked up, his usually stern face softening as he took in his daughter's flushed cheeks and glowing eyes.

"So how's the company morale?" he asked, setting aside the wooden spoon and crossing the room in two quick strides.

Delilah smiled. "Fantastic. Everyone's so happy! I love it!"

Abe grinned and gave her a hug.

A knot of tension unraveled within Delilah as she embraced her father. Overwhelmed by relief and love, she buried her face in his shoulder, feeling the comforting weight of his arms around her.

"Thank you, Dad." She pulled back to look him in the eye. "I couldn't have done it without everyone's support—especially yours."

"Family sticks together," Abe replied, a hint of a smile playing at the corners of his mouth. "We take care of each other, no matter what. That includes our friends and community. And nothing feels better than securing someone's livelihood." Abe's face lit up with pride. "You did a great job negotiating that deal."

As they stood there in the warmth of their kitchen, Delilah felt the last remnants of doubt and insecurity melt away. This was the connection she had been craving—the validation that her choices were as meaningful to him as they were to her.

"Promise me one thing, though," Abe said, his gaze serious but warm. "Don't forget to take care of yourself too, okay? You're just as important as everyone else."

Delilah nodded, blinking back tears. "I promise, Dad," she whispered, hugging him once more before stepping back.

As they returned to the stove, side by side, laughter and light-hearted conversation filling the air, Delilah's thoughts raced with newfound clarity. She had discovered the true value of community and connection, and learned that it was possible to honor both her father and herself in the process.

But what would happen next? How would this new chapter unfold for her and those around her? And what other challenges might lie ahead?

Whatever comes our way, she thought, taking a deep breath, *we'll face it head-on.*

With that resolve etched onto her soul, Delilah turned her attention back to her father, ready to embrace the future—and all its uncertainties—with open arms.

"There's one more thing that I feel I should tell you," Abe said, his voice solemn. "It's about Jobe's father."

CHAPTER 15

Delilah frowned, instantly on edge. She had known Jobe's family for years but had no idea what her father was referring to. "What is it?" she asked cautiously.

Abe sighed but then smiled broadly. "Several months ago," he began slowly, "Jobe's father invested in Alexandria Meat with the intention of saving it from going under."

Delilah stared at her father, the words he had spoken reverberating through her mind. Jobe's father had invested in Alexandria Meat? The revelation was a shock, illuminating connections she hadn't even considered before. Her hands shook slightly with the intensity of the emotions coursing through her.

"Wait," she stammered, trying to process the information. "Really?"

Abe nodded solemnly, his eyes filled with understanding and compassion. "Yes, Delilah. He saw the value in our community and wanted to help preserve it."

"Wow," Delilah murmured, her thoughts scrambling. She considered the implications of this newfound knowledge—how it connected her journey with Jobe's, and how their fathers' actions had inadvertently brought them closer. It was almost poetic in its symmetry, and she felt a sense of awe at the intricate tapestry of life that had been woven around them.

"Does Jobe know?" she asked, her voice barely a whisper.

Abe hesitated for a moment before replying. "No, I don't think so. I'm sure his father was going to tell him one day, but…"

Delilah felt a strong conviction fueled by the desire to honor both her father's wishes and the memory of Jobe's own father. "I want to tell him, Dad. It feels like the right thing to do."

It struck Delilah that she had something else important to tell Jobe. She had to tell him what she'd found out about the construction site—and the oil she'd found on the scaffold.

Abe gazed at Delilah for a long moment, then slowly nodded. "All right, if you think it's the right time, I trust your judgment."

"Thank you, Dad," she whispered, tears welling in her eyes as they embraced again. As she pulled away, Delilah knew that she was ready to face whatever consequences might arise from sharing this information with Jobe. It was a risk but one she felt compelled to take in order to honor the legacy of both their fathers.

CHAPTER 15

The next morning, with the sun's first light washing over the kitchen, Delilah breathed in deeply and faced her father.

Delilah's palms began to sweat as soon as she prepared to tell her father about her job offer in Europe. She had been anticipating this moment for days, yet now that it was here, she found herself filled with an uneasy mix of nervousness and reluctance.

But eventually, Delilah mustered up enough courage to speak.

"Remember those trips we took to Europe when I was a kid?" she began, her voice trembling. "Amsterdam was always my favorite…and…well…I've been offered a job there."

Abe's eyes widened in surprise, but he remained silent, waiting for her to continue.

"I want to take it, Dad," she said firmly, her eyes shining with determination. "I want to see the world, experience new things."

"Will you be happy there, Delilah?" Abe asked, his voice steady despite the news.

"I believe so, Dad," she replied. "I'll miss you and everyone here terribly, but this is my chance. This is the adventure I've always dreamed of."

"Then go," Abe said, his voice choked with emotion. "Follow your heart, my girl. But remember, no matter where you are in the world, you'll always have a home here."

As Delilah walked away from her father, she felt a mixture of fear and exhilaration. She was taking control of her life, just as her father had taught her. But what would this new chapter mean for her relationship with Jobe? *What even is my relationship with Jobe? I don't know, but I'll miss him more than anything.*

It's been 40 days since my father passed away.

JOBE ROSE FROM his bed, the morning sun casting long shadows across the room. He had spent the last month pouring himself into the construction of the church his father had dreamed of building. It was nearly finished now, and the sight of it filled him with a sense of peace and closure.

The air was cool and crisp as Jobe arrived at the construction site. He gazed at the church, its walls rising proudly against the sky, a testament to his father's vision and determination. Workers bustled around him, adding the final touches to the structure, their voices a symphony of progress and hope.

"Hey, boss!" Jonathan called out, his breath visible in the chilly air. "We'll be done here in no time!"

"Thanks, Jonathan," Jobe replied, smiling as he watched his friend's enthusiasm for the project. He was grateful for the support of his loyal friend throughout this challenging time.

Looking around, Jobe couldn't help but think of what his father would say if he could see the church now. He knew that his father would be proud of him for taking action and honoring his memory in this way. It was a small victory amidst the sea of grief, but it provided solace nonetheless.

As the sun continued to rise, bathing the church in its warm glow, Jobe felt a growing sense of peace. Despite the unanswered questions about his future and the challenges that lay ahead, he knew that he had done right by his father. In that moment, it was enough.

AS THE MORNING light continued to grow, Delilah approached the construction site, her breathing slighted with anticipation and anxiety. She clutched the edge of her scarf, biting her lip as she searched for Jobe among the workers. The brisk air tugged at her loose strands of hair, mirroring the whirlwind of emotions that threatened to consume her.

"Jobe!" she called.

He turned to face her, his eyes widening in surprise. "Delilah! What are you doing here?"

"I needed to talk to you," she said, her voice more robust now, filled with determination. As she stepped closer, she could see the faint trace of sorrow in Jobe's eyes, a testament to the hardships he had faced in recent weeks.

"Is everything okay?" Jobe asked her.

"Everything's...well, it's about to change," Delilah admitted, taking a deep breath before continuing. "I've been offered a job in Europe, in Amsterdam."

"Amsterdam?" Jobe repeated, his voice barely above a whisper. A mixture of emotions flickered across his face—shock, confusion, and something that looked like pain.

"Yeah," Delilah murmured, her eyes glistening with unshed tears. "It's an incredible opportunity, but it means I'll be leaving soon."

For a moment, neither of them spoke, Delilah's words hanging heavy in the air between them. Then, as if driven by an unseen force, they moved toward each other, their arms wrapping around one another in a tight embrace. They stood there, clinging to each other as the world continued to spin around them.

"Congratulations, Delilah," Jobe whispered into her ear, his voice thick with emotion.

"Thank you, Jobe," she replied, her voice muffled by his shoulder. "I'm going to miss you so much."

"I'm going to miss you too," he said warmly, holding her even tighter.

As they finally pulled apart, Jobe gazed into her eyes. He sought to say a thousand things to her, but he said nothing.

Delilah had been so caught up in telling Jobe she was going away that she nearly forgot she had other news to share with him. "Oh, Jobe," she started, a hand on his arm. "I have to tell you something else."

Jobe just looked at her, no doubt aware from her tone that this was serious.

"When we were at your father's funeral, I overheard someone talking about your father's accident. He suspected something intentional happened. Said someone might've done something to the scaffold."

Jobe's eyes looked as intense as Delilah had ever seen them. "What?"

"I had to find out more, so I went to the construction site to check it out. I climbed up the scaffold, and there was oil on the platform. It was so slippery."

Jobe was still gazing intently into Delilah's eyes.

"And then…Michelle said she saw Luke Belial snooping around the construction site the day of the accident. I don't know what it all means or if it's just coincidence, but I had to tell you."

A look of knowing passed over Jobe's face, where his eyes went wide as if he had just discovered something. Then his face went blank, and he nodded grimly.

"I'm sorry if I've upset you," said Delilah, and she squeezed his arm. "Don't worry, I've already told the police. I told them as soon as I found out. Michelle also told them what she saw. They're not sure if it actually means anything or not. I didn't want to tell you and get you all worked up if it turned out to be nothing."

"No, I understand," said Jobe. "Thanks for telling me. It's definitely strange, but as long as the police have the information, I'm sure they'll look into it further if..." he trailed off. He sat there in silence for a long moment.

Delilah smiled at him. "But there's happier news. Did you know your father invested in Alexandria Meat?"

Jobe looked nonplussed. "My father? He did?"

Delilah nodded heartily. "Yup. My father told me yesterday. Apparently, Alexandria Meat would've gone under a long time ago had it not been for your father."

Jobe smiled at this, his eyes watering. He looked all around—at the nearly-finished church, at the soft, green grass that grew in front of it—and then back at Delilah. "Let's plant a tree for him here."

"Plant a tree..." Delilah said. "Yes! That's a great idea."

"And then he'll always be with us," Jobe said with a smile. "He'll always be here right by his church."

"I love it," said Delilah, and she wrapped Jobe in another hug.

"And it can also represent us," Jobe said, pulling back and looking into her eyes. "We'll always have roots here, even if we're not here physically."

Delilah now felt the tears welling up in her own eyes, taken with emotion at Jobe's statement. "We'll always have roots here," she echoed. "Always."

They squeezed each other tight, rocking back and forth for a long moment.

CHAPTER 15

After the embrace, Delilah remembered the big oak tree growing outside Michelle's house. The last time she was there, acorns were falling, and she looked at Jobe excitedly and grinned. "How about an oak tree?"

Jobe beamed. "Let's do it!"

"Okay, come with me!" Delilah told him, and she marched to her car excitedly with Jobe at her heels.

Delilah drove them to Michelle's house, where a giant oak tree stood, and they got out of the car and stood underneath its branches. Looking down at their feet, a plethora of acorns were scattered about the ground—so many that they didn't know which one to pick.

"Can we plant any of these?" Delilah asked Jobe, gazing down at the myriad acorns at her feet.

Jobe squatted down, feeling the acorns that lie in the dirt. "Some of these are pretty dry," he said. "The fresher, the better."

And just as he said that, an acorn came free-falling down from the branches above, landing right in Delilah's crimson locks, then bouncing off and coasting toward the ground.

Jobe caught the acorn right before it struck the dirt, and he and Delilah laughed.

"That's about as fresh as it gets," said Jobe, still laughing.

"You're telling me." Delilah giggled. "So what's next?" she asked Jobe, assuming he knew more about planting trees than she did. And she was right.

"Well, we should start it in a pot," said Jobe, placing the acorn gently in his pocket. "Once it's sprouted and growing a little bit, we can put it in the ground. Has a better chance of surviving that way. If we put the acorn straight into the ground, it could be eaten up by mice or squirrels before it has a chance to grow."

Delilah marveled, not knowing Jobe was so knowledgeable in this area. It hurt her even more that she had to leave him.

As if Jobe could read her thoughts, he asked, "So when do you leave?"

"In a few weeks," said Delilah.

Jobe shone a smile at her. "Perfect. That should be just enough time. Once it's sprouted nice and strong, we can put it in the ground together."

And the thought of that made Delilah very, very happy.

Off they went to the hardware store, picking up a plant pot, potting soil, a small hand shovel, and chicken wire which Jobe said they'd need later. They filled the pot with soil, dug down about an inch, and placed the acorn sideways into the damp potting soil.

Weeks later, when the acorn had germinated and a bright green seedling emerged from the soil, Jobe and Delilah took the plant to its permanent place by the church. In the soft green grass in front of the building, they dug a small hole and carefully removed the seedling from its pot and placed it in its new earthen home.

Jobe built a barrier around it using chicken wire, protecting the young, vulnerable plant from animals that might eat it. Delilah looked down at the little seedling, feeling a sense of pride and accomplishment she didn't think could come from simply planting a tree. Best of all was the look on Jobe's face as he gazed down at the plant with pride.

"Thank you," he said, turning to face her. "Thanks for doing this with me."

"Of course," said Delilah, and she noticed a look in Jobe's eyes that made her heart skip a beat.

He stepped closer to her, took her cheek in his hand and kissed her.

Delilah was overwhelmed with feelings: happiness, sorrow, nervousness, regret—she felt them all. There was an even stronger feeling, or maybe it was a mix of all the other emotions, but she had to wonder if it was—

"Promise me one thing," Jobe said, taking both her hands in his. "Promise me that you'll make the most of this opportunity, that you'll live your life to the fullest."

"I promise," Delilah whispered, her eyes shining with the fire of determination. This was the start of something new, something that would change her life forever. Although the path ahead was filled with uncertainty, she had faith in her ability to face whatever challenges lay ahead.

With one last lingering look at each other, they stepped back, their hands slowly slipping apart with the final rays of the setting sun.

PATH BLOCKED

5

AS DELILAH STRODE through the bustling airport, she bubbled with anticipation and anxiety. The scent of coffee wafted through the air, mingling with the din of announcements and hurried conversations. Her fingers tightened around the handle of her suitcase, her knuckles white from the grip.

"Flight KL1729 to Amsterdam is now boarding at Gate 7!" the announcement rang out, its urgency amplifying throughout the waiting area.

Delilah sprinted through the crowded airport terminal, her suitcase bouncing wildly behind her. Her flight to Amsterdam was boarding, and she couldn't afford to miss it. Voices surrounded her, but one distinct voice caught her attention above the rest.

"Wait!" a man shouted from behind her. Delilah skidded to a halt, causing her suitcase to topple over. She turned to see a well-dressed man with piercing eyes jogging toward her. "You dropped this," he said, handing her a small leather-bound notebook.

"Thank you," Delilah said, tucking the notebook securely into her bag. The man flashed her a warm smile, his eyes twinkling with charisma. "I'm Jude, by the way."

"Delilah," she replied, shaking his outstretched hand. There was an immediate sense of connection between them, as though they'd known each other for years. "Are you on the flight to Amsterdam as well?"

"Indeed, I am," Jude said, glancing at his watch. "We should hurry, though. It's leaving soon."

They dashed toward the gate, their footsteps echoing in unison against the polished floor. They made it just in time, boarding passes in hand as they stepped onto the plane.

As the aircraft rumbled to life, Delilah gazed out the window, watching the ground slowly disappear beneath her. She thought about the steps she had taken to save Alexandria Meat, honoring her father and staying true to his values. Now, she was taking another bold step—not only for herself but also for those who had supported her along the way.

"Are you okay?" Jude asked, no doubt noticing her pensive expression.

"Actually, I'm more than okay," Delilah replied, a determined smile forming on her lips. "I'm ready for whatever comes next."

"Good," Jude said, giving her an encouraging nod. "That's the spirit."

Delilah leaned back in her seat, letting the hum of the engines wash away her worries. The thought of working in Europe filled her with a mixture of excitement and trepidation, but she was ready for the challenge. This was the opportunity she had been waiting for—an opportunity to make something special out of her life. Despite all the uncertainty, she was certain that this was what she had wanted all along—to take control of her destiny and realize her dreams.

She had manifested this moment, she thought with a smile, as well as fixing her broken relationship with her father.

It had started as a thought in her mind, a simple idea. Through action, she had molded it into reality. And here she was, catching a flight to work in Europe as she had always dreamed of, the relationship with her father intact and more beautiful than ever.

It made her think of the words her father used to tell her about taking action and realizing her dreams—words she was just now starting to understand—make it be so.

MAKE IT BE SO

BALD

PLEASE POST A REVIEW
ON AMAZON FOR ME.
IT CAN MATTER!

THANKS
BALD
S

Dear Pathfinders,

You've just turned the final pages of our latest adventure, and your mind is likely swirling with questions, thoughts, and emotions.

Welcome to Path Talk, a unique bonus chapter in which I step out of my role of author and move onto the pages to engage our characters in intimate, revealing conversations. I put down my pen to join our characters for banter you won't want to miss.

What makes Path Talk special? Depth and backstory.

It's an arena where you sit down with me as we explore the themes, events, and choices that helped shape the book you've just finished. It's one more vehicle for a richer understanding of the worlds you are exploring.

Think of yourself as a fly on the wall during a personal chat between friends. Today, this chat is between me and Jobe. This dialogue is meant to be private, full of emotion and unspoken truths. By reading this extra chapter, you're not just an observer but a privileged member of the Path Series™ inner circle.

I trust that you will like this.

BALD

Bald Solomon: Jobe, there's something quite enchanting about that oak tree you and Delilah planted near the church. Would you share the story behind it?

Jobe: Ah, the oak tree. It holds a special place for me. It's more than just a tree, it's a symbol of hope, love, and connection. You see, Delilah's parents planted a tree together on their wedding day. It marked the start of their journey together, something to watch grow and flourish, just like their love. But as time passed, they grew apart, and eventually, they divorced. Yet, that tree remained where they planted it, a silent witness to their ongoing story. As they used to tell me, "You plant a tree for the generations you'll never see."

Bald Solomon: It's a bittersweet memory. And now, with you and Delilah planting a tree together, it's life coming full circle.

Jobe: Exactly! When Delilah agreed to plant that tree with me, it felt like the universe was giving us a sign that new beginnings were possible, almost a rebirth. This tree and the church grounds it is growing on give me a place to remember and honor my dad. At the same time, it also represents Delilah's and my personal growth and deep friendship. We've faced challenges, but like that tree, we're determined to stand tall and thrive. Every time we see it, it reminds us of the beauty and strength of love.

Bald Solomon: Jobe, another moment in Path Unguided also resonated with me—when Delilah confronted her fears and took the lead to save Alexandria Meat. It felt like a significant turning point. Could you share your thoughts on that?

Jobe: Certainly. That moment truly showcases Delilah's courage and personal growth. She had been grappling with her broken relationship with her father and the weight of her past decisions.

When she chose to step up, it wasn't just about rescuing the plant; it was a step toward reconciling with her own conflict. Her determination to honor Abe's legacy and mend their relationship mirrored her commitment to rescuing Alexandria Meat. She recognized that taking action isn't just about external results; it's about finding her path and purpose.

Bald Solomon: And she didn't undertake this journey alone. You've been there beside her throughout. Your dedication to completing the church project in memory of your father adds another layer to the narrative.

Jobe: Absolutely. The church project goes way beyond just the construction of a building; it's a way for me to honor my father's memory and find closure. It's a way to finish what he couldn't. It's become a place where I can connect with him despite his absence.

The church project, planting the tree, saving Alexandria Meat—all three of these actions really represent the same thing. Grief isn't just about mourning; it's about discovering ways to honor those we've lost. That's what Delilah and I are both trying to do—find purpose amid the pain.

Bald Solomon: Jobe, shifting gears for a moment, let's talk about Luke Belial. He's quite a complex antagonist, wouldn't you agree?

Jobe: Indeed. Luke embodies the darker aspects of ambition and manipulation. He's a looming shadow, constantly lurking and attempting to disrupt the positive changes Delilah and I are working so hard to achieve.

Bald Solomon: What do you believe motivates someone like Luke? It seems there's a personal drive behind his actions.

Jobe: From what I've gathered, Luke's primary motivation appears to be personal financial gain. He aims to capitalize on the community's vulnerability and profit from it. He's an opportunist—a greedy one—with malicious intent.

Bald Solomon: So, he's willing to obstruct Delilah's mission for his own benefit. It's incredible how personal ambition can blind someone to the consequences of their actions on others.

Jobe: Unfortunately, that's the harsh reality. Luke's ambition has blinded him to the impact of his decisions on the community and the people who rely on the plant for their livelihoods. He's ready to sacrifice that for personal wealth. At times, Luke doesn't seem to even have a soul – almost the devil himself.

It's a sharp contrast to what drives me and Delilah. Our intentions are rooted in honoring our fathers' legacies and positively influencing the community. Our motivations stem from love, growth, and a sense of connection. We're striving to heal and uplift, while Luke seems driven solely by self-interest.

Bald Solomon: It's a fascinating dynamic, the clash between self-serving ambition and the desire to create a better future.

Jobe: That's the beauty of the Path Series™. All conflicts, whether internal or external, compel us to confront our values, fears, and desires and take action toward personal growth. It mirrors real life, where we all grapple with such complexities.

Bald Solomon: Let's shift our focus one more time. Something has been quietly present throughout many of the Path Series™ books. It's clear that there's a deep, unspoken connection between you and Delilah, something that carries a profound weight. Can you share your thoughts on this?

Jobe: You're absolutely right. Delilah and I share a history that goes way back, and as the years have passed, our relationship has evolved into something intricate and layered. There's a bond between us that defies easy description.

I think it's a combination of shared experiences, a deep mutual understanding, and a profound comfort in each other's presence. We've weathered many storms together, and that shared history forges a connection that's difficult to replicate.

Bald Solomon: Yet, there are many times when both of you hesitate to express your feelings. Is there something that holds you back?

Jobe: Fear plays a big role. We each carry our own baggage, our own insecurities. We've tiptoed around our emotions because we're afraid of risking what we already have, concerned that it might alter the dynamics between us.

I've clearly thought about this a lot. Part of me wonders if taking that step could bring us even closer or if it might complicate things irreparably. It's a risk I haven't been willing to take thus far.

Bald Solomon: Relationships inherently involve risk, Jobe, but they are among life's most beautiful and rewarding experiences. Sometimes, stepping out of our comfort zones and expressing our feelings can lead to growth and deeper connections.

Jobe: You are right. The path ahead may be uncertain, but with your guidance and the lessons I've learned, I'm more willing to explore what the future might hold for Delilah and me. Perhaps it's time for us to consider the possibility of growing together.

Bald Solomon: I'm glad to hear that. As Michelle might remind us, life's most profound moments often arise from following your heart. May your journey with Delilah continue to unfold, leading you both to deeper levels of connection and understanding.

Jobe, as we conclude the chapters of *Path Unguided*, I can't help but acknowledge the physical challenges you've recently faced. Although we never mention your injuries, your work as a firefighter has left its mark. How are you holding up?

Jobe: It's been quite the journey, Bald Solomon. My injuries have taken their toll on me, both physically and mentally. They serve as a stark reminder of the risks of my job and the strength required to work in this field.

It's been a process of adjustment and learning, to say the least. I've had to find ways to work around my injuries while still being effective in my role. The support I've received from my colleagues within the fire department has been invaluable on this journey.

Bald Solomon: Being a firefighter isn't just a job for you; it's a service. Yet, I can't help but wonder if these recent challenges are causing you to reconsider your future.

Jobe: You're absolutely right. My pains and injuries have forced me to confront the harsh reality that firefighting might not be sustainable for me in the long run.

Considering how this profession resonates with me, it's a challenging realization.

Bald Solomon: Your recognition is spot on. It reminds us that our paths are never rigidly set; they remain fluid and adaptable, just as life itself does. We will explore this theme explicitly with you in our next book on the Path Series™, Path Blocked.

Jobe: Cool. Although I admit I am a bit hesitant, I look forward to what lies ahead for me. Indeed, life is a tapestry woven with unexpected twists and turns, and I need to be more open to embracing them to continue forging ahead. Your support means a great deal to me. I'm excited to see where our shared path leads next.

I've shared quite a bit about my journey; let me turn it around to you. I'm curious about your journey as the author behind the Path Series™. What motivated you to write this impactful series?

Bald Solomon: Thank you so much for asking. As those who know me will attest, I love to talk about the Path Series™ and its impact on people's lives!

I was inspired to create the Path Series™ by witnessing people's triumphs and struggles, often resulting from their choices when facing common life challenges.

There are everyday events that occur in most people's lives. We fall in love. Our hearts get broken. We have a child. That child grows up. We lose our parents. We get old and frail. Importantly, these same human experiences have been going on for generations and generations around the world.

These events—and our actions surrounding these events—become critical junctions that bend the arc of our lives. So I have created the Path Series™ as a self-reflection tool to mentor each reader starting from where they are right now in life. Each Path Series™ book encourages the reader to personally reflect and then take action based on the combined wisdom of those who came before us.

I knew I needed a narrative that could resonate with readers, allowing them to see aspects of themselves in the characters' journeys. Developing the nuances of the characters' emotions and motivations involves crafting each character's unique backstory, experience, and desire. I want readers to connect their own struggles and triumphs with the characters, creating a layered, multi-dimensional narrative. It's about empathy and appreciating each character's personal growth.

I know the Path Series™ can make a difference in people's lives. Make it be so.

MAKE IT BE SO

BALD

PATH TALK

Prequel Summary:

Path Series™ Book 6
Path Divided: Surviving Divorce

Plunge into the impending chaos that is the marriage of Abe and Lydia Boaz. Their once-storybook union now teeters on the brink, strained by financial turmoil and heartbreaking communication breakdowns.

Lydia, the sharp-witted CFO of Alexandria Meat, battles the company's dire financial straits, while the powerful businessman Abe remains stubbornly blind to their reality. When their union finally shatters, Lydia flees to a fresh start in New York City, only to be ensnared by a faceless stalker who creates a nightmarish world of fear and paranoia.

Abe reluctantly steps in to protect his now ex-wife, Lydia, fearing for their vulnerable daughter, Delilah. The suspense escalates, and the enigmatic stalker remains elusive. Dive into the characters' innermost fears and vulnerabilities as they evolve and grow as a newly divided family.

Bald Solomon delivers another fast moving Path Series™ journey of transformation, resilience, and unbreakable bonds.

Sequel Summary:

Path Series™ Book 8
Path Blocked: Overcoming Unemployment

Haunted by his firefighting past, Jobe Johnson lives aimlessly, mired in unemployment and self-doubt. His life takes an exciting turn when an anonymous letter promises a new path.

Delilah Boaz, Jobe's lost love, unexpectedly returns to Alexandria with her mysterious new boyfriend, Jude, clouding Jobe's mind with memories and jumbled thoughts.

Amidst the relentless flooding of the Gozan River, Jobe must save his hometown of Alexandria. Surrounded by this chaos and turmoil, Jobe discovers opportunity and creates his future.

As with his other Path Series™ books, Bald Solomon weaves a captivating action story of inner conflict, community struggle, and personal growth.

MAKE IT BE SO BALD

Vantage Point

Here are some points to ponder as you grieve for your father.

1. How am I feeling right now? What does my grief feel like now?
2. How do I feel about my relationship with my dad?
3. What are some special memories I have of my dad? What words did he use or habits did he have?
4. What lessons did I learn from my dad?
5. What emotions have been most prominent for me since my dad died?
6. How has my daily life changed since my dad died?
7. What am I struggling with or find particularly challenging?
8. Do I have any unresolved issues or unfinished conversations? Who could I share these with?
9. What rituals or activities might help me cope with my grief?
10. How could I take better care of myself while I grieve?
11. How might I honor my dad's memory?

Terminus

"Grief is the price we pay for love."

—Queen Elizabeth II

PATH TALK

Made in USA - North Chelmsford, MA
46905_9781962821094
12.18.2023 1341